LECKIE
the education publisher
for Scotland

National 5
BUSINESS MANAGEMENT

Course Notes

Dr Lee Coutts

ISBN 9780008461188

Published by
Leckie
An imprint of HarperCollins Publishers
Westerhill Road, Bishopbriggs, Glasgow, G64 2QT
T: 0844 576 8126 F: 0844 576 8131
leckiescotland@harpercollins.co.uk   www.leckiescotland.co.uk

HarperCollins Publishers
Macken House, 39/40 Mayor Street Upper, Dublin 1, D01 C9W8, Ireland

Special thanks to
Jill Laidlaw (copyeditor and proofreader)
Delphine Lawrance (picture research)
Pam Oates (content review)

A CIP Catalogue record for this book is available from the British Library.

Acknowledgements
We would like to thank the following for permission to reproduce their material:
page 4 photo © wavebreakmedia; page 8-9 photo © Sergey Nivens / Shutterstock.com; page 10 photo © Thinkstock; page 11 photo © Ariwasabi; page 11 photo © baranq; page 14 photo Chiyacat; page 17 photo © Elena Elisseeva; page 17 photo © Dmitry Kalinovsky; page 17 photo © pjcross; page 18 Case study (logo) © Sorted; page 22 photo © Thinkstock; page 23 photo © Angelina Dimitrova; page 24 © crown copyright; page 28 photo © Ioannis Pantzi; page 30 Case study (logo) © Lee Coutts; page 33 photo © 1000 Words; page 34 photo © Anton Oparin; page 35 photo © michaeljung; page 37 Case study (photo) © Simpsons Garden Centre; page 39 photo © mikeledray; page 40 photo © Getty Images/Jupiterimages; page 48-49 photo © everything possible / Shutterstock.com; page 51 photo © Cheryl Savan; page 52 graph © Statista.com; page 55 photo © scyther5; page 56 photo © Shutterstock.com; page 61 logo © Heinz; page 61 logo © McDonald's used with permission from McDonald's Restaurants Limited; page 67 photo © Tupungato; page 67 photo © Ivan Kruk; page 67 photo © Pierre-Yves Babelon; page 67 photo © Rafael Ramirez Lee; page 68 photo © Spectral-Design; page 70 photo © rvlsoft; page 74 photo © Thinkstock; page 76 Case study (logo) © Reactive Training; page 77 photo © mama_mia; page 80 photo © Yuri Arcurs; page 80 photo © Rido; page 80 photo © Monkey Business Images; page 80 logo © Twitter; page 86 photo © Olaf Speier; page 89 photo © Andrey Burmakin; page 90 photo © Katrina Brown; page 91 photo © Olaf Speier; page 91 photo © chinahbzyg; page 92 photo © Alexander Sayenko; page 94 photo © kongsky; page 95 Case study (photo and text) © Mackie's Ice Cream; page 102-103 photo © Wright Studio / Shutterstock.com; page 109 photo © Monkey Business Images; page 111 photo © dotshock; page 112 photo © Pressmaster; page 116 photo © godrick; page 117 photo © wavebreakmedia; page 117 minimum wage figures © www.gov.uk; page 123 photo © StockCube; page 128 © Phonlamai Photo / Shutterstock.com; page 130 photo © Lim Yong Hian

Printed in Great Britain by Ashford Colour Press Ltd.

Chapter 1

UNIT 1 – Understanding Business

Chapter 2

Chapter 3

End of unit material

UNIT 2 – Management of Marketing and Operations

Chapter 4

Chapter 5

End of unit material   98

UNIT 3 – Management of People and Finance

Chapter 6

Chapter 7

End of unit material   137

Answers   141

1 Get set for learning

What you will learn in this chapter

- The structure of this book.
- The structure of the National 5 Business Management course.

Welcome to your course notes

These course notes have been written with only you in mind and are designed to help you achieve the most from this course. This book encourages you to think about your learning and to develop Skills for Learning, Life and Work.

There are 5 areas of study in National 5 Business Management, and each area of study has at least one chapter dedicated to it in this book:

- Understanding Business (chapter 2 and 3)
- Management of Marketing (chapter 4)
- Management of Operations (chapter 5)
- Management of People (chapter 6)
- Management of Finance (chapter 7)

Depending on the school or college where you are undertaking this qualification, you might have formal assessments to sit after each area of study.

Structure of this book

The structure of this book is the same throughout.

At the beginning of each unit, there is an introductory section explaining what you will learn in that unit.

Each chapter begins with a list of what you should already know (perhaps from National 4 Business or from your education in S1–S3) and a list of learning intentions; this is what you will learn in that chapter. Throughout each chapter there are a number of activities, quick questions, case studies and key questions for you to answer.

- **Activities** are designed to allow you to apply the knowledge you have just learned in different situations. You will do these either individually, in pairs, in groups or as a class. Each activity has a list of skills that the activity will develop.

Some of the topics you will learn about on this Business Management course

These skills will be very useful to you not just in this course, but for life, work and future learning. See page 6 for further information.

- **Quick questions** are designed to test your knowledge of what you have learned. Some questions are easier than others but they give you the opportunity to think about what you have learned.

- **Case studies** are all real examples of businesses based in Scotland. They contain a short amount of text to read, followed by questions. These case studies are excellent preparation for your course assessment because they get you thinking carefully about the business under discussion and looking at the case study for answers.

- **Key questions** confirm that you have grasped the main points of the chapter. Being able to answer these should help you feel confident for the unit assessment.

At the end of each area of study, you will find sample **exam-style questions** (with comments from an experienced examiner) and a traffic-light **self-assessment checklist**. *Please remember, depending on the school or college where you are undertaking this qualification, you might not have unit assessments to undertake. However, these course notes provide some guidance on what the unit assessment will contain if you are having to do these.*

Throughout the book there are **Watch points** that provide you with advice to help your learning and **Make the link** boxes that try to get you to connect what you are learning to other parts of the course and to other subjects.

These course notes contain lots of opportunities for you to work with other people, to use technology and to be creative. They will allow you to learn as much as you can.

A blog is a popular way of keeping notes

Your learning journal

You will be asked to keep a learning journal throughout your National 5 Business Management course. This journal is not part of your formal assessment but will get you thinking about your learning and is a place where you can keep different things you have learned. It will help you to develop your literacy and communication skills as well as to improve your knowledge of Business Management.

Your learning journal could take a number of formats – you can decide how you want it to look. You might simply use a jotter to record things and stick things into or you might have a folder you could use. You could also keep a blog or journal online that records what you are learning.

At various points in this book you are given prompts to record things in your journal but in addition to this you should:

- Keep copies of relevant newspaper articles or internet printouts/screen shots that you have read or seen. Write down next to each one why it was relevant and what you learned from it.

- Write about what you have heard on the news that is relevant to what you are learning in Business Management. Make a note about the report you listened to and what you learned from it.

- Record when you have engaged with a real business as part of your course, for example if your class visited a business or if you had a guest speaker talking to your class. Note down what you learned and what you enjoyed.

- Make a list of key words/concepts that you have learned in class and what these mean – this will make an excellent revision tool for revising for assessments. You should add to your list after every Business Management class.

Your learning journal will be something you can look at throughout your course and you could even take it to a job or college interview to show them what you have been learning.

The first task for your learning journal appears on page 7.

National 5 Business Management

Business Management is relevant to everybody – no matter what route their life takes. We all come into contact with business on a daily basis, from using public transport, to buying something in a shop, to watching the TV. Business has a powerful influence and impact on us, the economy and the world. This course will enable you to understand how businesses operate and the activities they undertake. It will also develop your employability and enterprise skills.

For those still at school, National 5 Business Management aims to build on the knowledge and skills learned in social studies and technologies in S1–S3. For those not at school, the course will introduce you to the main concepts and topics within the modern business world. Some learners may have studied National 4 Business before undertaking this course and this provides an excellent foundation for studying at National 5.

National 5 is at Scottish Credit and Qualifications Framework (SCQF) level 5 and this course is worth 24 SCQF credit points. SCQF is the name given to the framework used to describe qualifications in Scotland. SCQF level 5 describes the level of difficulty of the course and the points are how long the course will take to complete with 1 point = ten hours of learning. Every National 5 course is at SCQF level 5 and contains 24 credit points.

Assessment

Your teacher will provide you with feedback regularly to let you know how well you understand the topics in the course. You will also get the opportunity to receive feedback from your peers and to reflect on your own learning. Your learning journal can be used to track your progress throughout the course and you can record your feelings and experiences as you go along.

Because this course is certificated by the Scottish Qualifications Authority (SQA), you have to undertake formal assessments that will be used to demonstrate that you have achieved each learning outcome as well as the overall course aims.

Unit assessment

Some of you might have to sit assessments at the end of each area of study, depending on the school or college you are in. Your teacher or lecturer will tell you if this applies to you and what you are required to do.

Course assessment

The course assessment allows you to show that you have achieved the aims of the course and for you to demonstrate added value. Added value means that you are able to use your knowledge and skills in different and sometimes challenging situations. The course assessment provides you with an overall grade (A–D or No Award) for the National 5 Business Management course. The grade is based on the overall mark you achieve for the course assessment out of 100.

You will have to sit an exam as part of your assessment for Business Management

The course assessment for National 5 Business Management consists of two parts:

Question paper This is worth 90 marks of the course assessment	This is an end-of-course exam. The exam is set and marked by the SQA. It is a closed-book exam and you will not know in advance which topics will be assessed. The exam will last 2 hours.
Assignment This is worth 30 marks of the course assessment	The assignment will require you to prepare a short report on a specific area (eg technology, finance, quality, recruitment) of a business you have chosen. You will have to show that you can plan, research and make decisions when undertaking the assignment and use different sources of information.

Skills for Learning, Life and Work

Throughout your course and this book, you are given opportunities to develop Skills for Learning, Life and Work. These are general skills that you need for your future. The **Activities** in this book are designed to address a number of skills and these are highlighted. These will also help prepare you for the course assessment. The skills you will develop are:

Numeracy	This involves using numbers and creating/interpreting graphical information. This is mainly developed in the Finance chapter of this book.
Employability	These are work-related skills that employers are looking for. These skills are also about helping you to become more familiar with the different careers and opportunities available to you.
ICT	This involves using technology for learning. You will be given the opportunity to use lots of technology to help you learn, including modern technologies such as Web 2.0 and mobile technologies.
Thinking	This involves thinking about an issue and the impact or consequences it might have. It also involves reflecting on something you have done and thinking about how well it went.
Decision making	This means making a choice. You might be presented with information and have to make a choice. When making decisions, you should be able to give reasons for your choice.

Enterprise	This skill is about being creative and coming up with new ideas. It involves applying what you have learned to new and innovative contexts.
Communication	This means being able to talk to other people. You might be asked to do this in writing or orally but both are equally important. You need to be able to put your point of view across and to present facts. You also need to be able to listen to other views. When communicating, you should use appropriate business terms as often as you can.
Research	This skill involves finding things out. This might mean using a number of sources such as the internet, books or people. You should use good quality sources of information and you will learn how to evaluate them. Remember, not all sources of information contain correct facts and you will learn to question the reliability of information. This skill will be important when you undertake your assignment for this course.

GO! Activity

You are required to keep a learning journal throughout your Business Management course. Page 4 provides more information about what this should contain. To get started you should:

1. Decide what format your learning journal will take (will it be a jotter, a folder or electronically, using a blog or journal?).
2. Start your learning journal by creating a front cover or setting up your blog/journal ready for you to write in.

When your learning journal is ready to be used, you should answer the following questions:

1. Why have you chosen the format for your journal that you did?
2. What do you want to get out of studying Business Management?
3. How will you try to achieve what you want to get from the course?

Remember, your learning journal is a record of your learning journey throughout this course. This book contains prompts to remind you to record things, but you should feel free to write as much as you can about your learning in Business Management. Your teacher will ask to see your learning journal on a regular basis to make sure you are keeping it up-to-date and professional.

Skills

- Decision making
- Thinking
- ICT

1

Understanding Business

2 The business environment

You should already be able to

- Outline reasons for individuals setting up in business.
- Describe the skills and attributes needed by entrepreneurs when setting up a business.
- Outline features of a small business.
- Describe sources of finance and support when setting up a small business.

What you will learn in this chapter

- The role of business
- Types of business organisations
- Customer satisfaction
- Objectives

The role of business

We might not realise it, but business is all around us; when we walk down the street, when we watch television and when we go on holiday. We need businesses to be able to live, work and play.

Look at the following list of activities and think about which ones you have done today already.

- Had toast for breakfast
- Styled your hair
- Taken the bus or train
- Used a mobile phone to send a text message
- Watched the news on TV

The chances are you have done some of these things and each of them involves business. If you had toast for breakfast, a farmer had to grow the crop to be able to make flour. This flour was then used by the baker, along with other ingredients to make the bread, before being put into the oven to bake. Once baked, the bread was then sliced and put into packaging before being transported by lorry to a shop. Once it arrived at the shop it was unpacked and placed carefully on the shelf before you came along (or someone else came along for you) and bought the bread. As you can see, each stage, from farmer to baker to shop, involves business. Sometimes people underestimate how important and powerful business is but without it we wouldn't be able to do lots of things.

Businesses provide us with things that we need to go about our daily lives.

We all have things that we **need** to live and things that we **want** to have.

I **need** water, food, clothing and shelter to be able to live.

I **want** a new mobile phone and I **want** to go on holiday this summer.

Needs are essential for us to be able to live and include water, clothing, food and shelter. **Wants** are things that we would like to have, but can live without. We can live without a mobile phone, television and holidays, but we couldn't live without food or water.

Goods and services

Businesses **produce** goods and services to help us satisfy our needs and wants. We satisfy our needs and wants by **consuming** (using up) the different goods and services that they produce.

Goods are things we can see, touch and pick up. This means goods are tangible. Examples of goods are DVDs, a chocolate bar, clothes and a newspaper. Some goods are **durable** (can be used more than once) such as a washing machine, whereas some are **non-durable** (can't be used more than once) such as a plaster.

Services are things we can't see, touch or pick up. This means they are intangible. Services are usually provided by people who have been trained to supply them. For example, getting a haircut from a hairdresser, getting a tooth filled by a dentist or getting a mechanic to fix a car. Services are usually provided by people who are trained in carrying out a specific task.

Some businesses provide us with goods and services. For example, Greggs the Bakers will sell us a sausage roll (providing a good) but if we ask for it, they will heat it up (providing a service).

Make the link

The marketing function of a business spends a lot of time and money trying to find out what we want to buy and what we get satisfaction from consuming. Marketing carries out market research, eg a survey or interviews, and then uses this information to produce a product that we want, and will hopefully make the business a profit.

This business cycle diagram summarises what we have learned so far and how it links together.

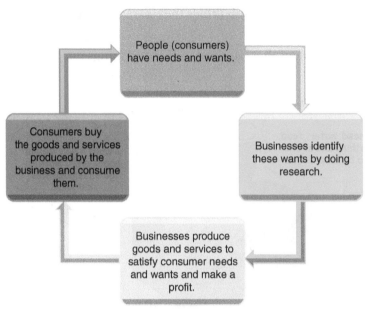

The business cycle

? Questions

1. What is the difference between a need and a want?
2. Give two examples of a need.
3. Give two examples of a want.
4. What two groups of people might not have all their needs satisfied?
5. What is the difference between a good and a service?
6. From the list below, identify which items are goods and which items are services.

A computer	Internet access	Newspaper
TV programme	Can of juice	Getting a haircut
A train journey	Being taught	CD

7. What is the difference between a durable and non-durable good?
8. What does the term 'production' mean?
9. What does the term 'consumption' mean?
10. How do businesses find out what the needs and wants of people are?
11. Give one reason why a business wants to satisfy people's needs and wants.

GO! Activity

Make a list of careers you might be interested in that involve providing a service.

Using the My World of Work website, find out more about one of these careers and the tasks and responsibilities associated with it. Make a list of the qualifications and skills that you need to do the job. Think about how your knowledge of Business Management will help you in this job. (Remember, we all come into contact with business so knowledge of Business Management helps everyone.)

In your learning journal, choose one of the jobs that really interest you. Write down why it interests you and think about what you would need to do to be able to do that job.

- Employability
- Thinking

Factors of production

To provide us with products (goods and services), businesses have to co-ordinate the factors of production. Factors of production are the different resources that are combined to produce something.

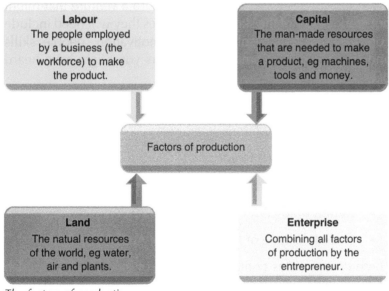

Labour
The people employed by a business (the workforce) to make the product.

Capital
The man-made resources that are needed to make a product, eg machines, tools and money.

Factors of production

Land
The natual resources of the world, eg water, air and plants.

Enterprise
Combining all factors of production by the entrepreneur.

The factors of production

We can apply what we have learned about the factors of production to an example so that we can understand it better. Let's look at the factors of production and how they combine to make jeans.

Land

Cotton is harvested from plants (a natural resource) and is used to make denim.

Capital

Sewing machines, irons and indigo (the chemical used to make jeans blue) are used in the production process. These are all man-made resources.

Labour

Workers have to sew different parts of the denim together.

Enterprise

The entrepreneur has to come up with the idea for the jeans and combine the factors of production, eg Levi Strauss is the entrepreneur behind Levi jeans.

The factors of production combine to produce a pair of jeans

⚠ Watch point

Remember the mnemonic CELL: Capital, Enterprise, Land, Labour.

GO! Activity

In groups, you are required to:

- Make a list of all the skills and qualities an entrepreneur might have and then;
- Suggest at least one reason why each skill or quality would be important for the success of the business.
- You can do this either as a graffiti wall or as a wiki.

In your learning journal, write down how entrepreneurial you are – what enterprising skills and qualities do you have? How do you know you have these qualities?

The factors of production are combined by the entrepreneur. The entrepreneur is the person who is willing to take the risk to see whether or not his or her idea will work. Becoming a successful entrepreneur is not an easy task; they need to have lots of different skills and qualities, and have to be able to make decisions and invest money and time into a venture that might not work. Some of the skills and qualities they will need include confidence, problem-solving skills, motivation, people skills and determination. Some entrepreneurs you might have heard of include:

- Richard Branson (Virgin Group)
- Jo Malone (Jo Malone fragrances)
- James Dyson (Dyson)
- Bill Gates (Microsoft)
- Karren Brady (Vice Chairman of West Ham United)
- Steve Jobs (one of the founders of Apple)

These course notes contain a number of examples of Scottish entrepreneurs who have combined the factors of production and taken a risk.

🌳 Skills

- Enterprise
- Thinking
- Decision making
- Communication

GO! Activity

In groups, identify 3 skills or qualities an entrepreneur may have. Then, for each skill or quality, give a reason how that it may help a business organisation develop. (Hint think about why that skill or quality the entrepreneur has would help the business develop).

GO! Activity

The Prince's Scottish Youth Business Trust (PSYBT) provides support to young people in Scotland who want to set up new businesses.

Access the Prince's Scottish Youth Business Trust website and carry out the following tasks:

1. Make a list of information and any support provided.
2. Look at a minimum of two case studies and record the following in your learning journal:
   » Who started the business?
   » What does the business do?
   » Why is the business of interest to you?

Make the link

Some of the case studies used in these course notes can be found on the PSYBT website.

- Research
- Thinking
- Decision making

Wealth creation

Wealth is created by a business by adding value to a product as it goes through the production process. When jeans are being made, they go through the following chain of production.

As the jeans move from one stage of production to another, **wealth is being created**.

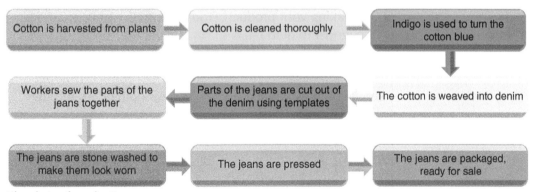

The chain of production

This is because **value is being added** to the price that will be charged by the business for the product. We will look at pricing products in marketing later in this textbook (see pages 62–64).

Think about it . . . the jeans are worth more as a finished product than as a collection of raw materials (cotton, indigo, buttons, zip, etc.) sitting in a pile. Another example would be building a house; as the house gets built it is worth more than the bricks, wood and paint sitting on an empty piece of land doing nothing.

Make the link

Production is covered in more detail in Chapter 5 (Operations). You will learn about different ways of producing products and how to make sure they are high quality.

GO! Activity

Your teacher/lecturer will put you into small groups and will allocate each group one of the following products.
Complete the tasks that follow.

- A bird house
- A car
- A chocolate bar
- A bag of crisps
- A pizza

Remember, everyone has a responsibility to participate in a group task sensibly. It's time to take control of your learning and get thinking. Appoint a group leader to make sure everyone contributes and works within the time given by your teacher/lecturer.

Task 1
Identify whether the product you have been given is durable or non-durable, giving a reason for your answer.

Task 2
Apply the four factors of production to your product. Can you list the land, labour, capital and enterprise that went into making your product? (You can use the jeans example on page 14 to help.)

Task 3
Create the chain of production for your product. This will show you how value is added as the product goes through different stages.

Task 4
Once you have finished this task, be prepared to present your findings to the class. Your class will judge how useful each advert is and will give feedback on:

- **The information communicated**, eg description of the product, how well you have applied the factors of production, the information in your chain of production.
- **The level of teamwork displayed**. You should make sure each member of the group participates and has a role to play when presenting your advert.

You should write down in your learning journal how you think this task went: What went well? What didn't? How would you rate your contribution? What leadership and employability skills did you use?

Skills

- Communication
- Thinking
- Enterprise

Sectors of industry

We know that businesses combine the factors of production to produce goods and services and in doing so, satisfy the needs and wants of consumers.

Businesses belong to different sectors of industry: primary, secondary or tertiary.

Primary	Secondary	Tertiary
Businesses in this sector take raw materials from the ground, eg agriculture and farming, fishing, mining.	Businesses in this sector use raw materials and make something with them, eg a car manufacturer, a builder, a cake baker.	Businesses in this sector provide a service, eg a fitness instructor, a hotel, a supermarket.

GO! Activity

This is a 'speed dating' activity to do with sectors of industry. This activity works best if you can get access to a large empty space such as a sports or assembly hall.

- Think of a career you are interested in.
- Walk round all your classmates individually and ask them what career they are interested in. When they tell you, you have to say what sector of industry (or industries) their career belongs to. They can then ask you what career you are interested in and it is their turn to tell you which sector of industry your chosen career belongs to.

Write down in your learning journal what career you are interested in and which sector of industry it belongs to.

Make the link

Some businesses will belong to more than one industry sector. For example, a farmer might harvest his own fruit, bake this fruit into a cake and then sell the cake in a farm shop. In this example, the farmer's business would belong to all three sectors.

- Communication
- Employability

🔍 Case study

SORTED, Aberdeenshire

Lorne Thomson has his own business, called Sorted, that can arrange and provide everything you need for a great party. It is based in Aberdeenshire and aims to offer the highest possible customer service. Lorne started Sorted in 2011 and offers his product to parties, weddings, christenings and other events. Sorted can provide everything you need from decorations and displays to chocolate fountains, balloons and candy bars.

❓ Questions

1. Does Sorted provide a good or a service? Give a reason for your answer.
2. Which sector of industry does Sorted belong to?
3. Lorne is an entrepreneur. What is an entrepreneur?
4. What skills and qualities do entrepreneurs like Lorne have?
5. Where might Lorne's business idea have come from?
6. Suggest two risks Lorne took when setting up his business.
7. Suggest an aim of Sorted.

? Questions

1. What does the term 'factors of production' mean?
2. Name the four factors of production.
3. Describe each factor of production.
4. Who combines the factors of production?
5. Name three skills an entrepreneur might have.
6. What does the term 'creating wealth' mean?
7. Name and describe the sectors of industry.
8. From the list below, name the sector of industry each business would belong to:

Tourist Information Centre	Forfar Potato Farmer
Scottish Exhibition & Conference Centre	Hilton Hotel
Arbroath Smokie Farmer	Clyde Shipbuilders
Stirling Builders	O2

Types of business organisations

There are lots of different businesses and they provide a range of different goods and services. We can group these goods and services into three categories, called sectors of the economy. Within each sector of the economy there are different types of businesses. In this course we concentrate on small to medium-sized businesses.

> **⚠ Watch point**
>
> The sectors of the economy (private, public, third) are different from sectors of industry (primary, secondary, tertiary).

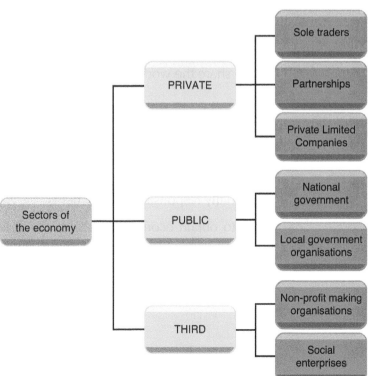

Sectors of the economy

Private sector

Private sector organisations are owned by individuals and aim to make a profit.

	Sole trader	Partnership	Private Limited Company
What is it?	A business owned by one person.	A business owned by 2–20 people.	A company owned by people who have been invited to buy shares.
Who owns it?	The sole trader	The partners	The shareholders
Who runs it?	The sole trader	The partners	Board of Directors
Examples	Rob Jackson Joinery	Adams & McNeill Accountants	Fly High Travel Ltd

⚠ Watch point

A good way to remember the different types of business is to think about who owns and who controls it.

Sole traders are usually small businesses and are a popular choice when people are starting up a business. Normally the sole trader would invest his or her own money (this is known as capital) into the business when starting it up.

The advantages of being a sole trader are:

- Easy to set up; do not need to complete lots of legal documents.

- All of the profits are kept by the owner.

- The owner can choose when to work and when to take holidays.

- All the decisions are made by the owner and can be made quickly without having to consult other people.

The disadvantages of being a sole trader are:

- There is nobody to share the workload and responsibility with.

- Raising large amounts of start-up capital can be difficult as the business might be seen as more of a risk compared to a larger, more established business.

- Unlimited liability – this means if the business fails, the sole trader is personally responsible for any debts.

- It can be difficult to obtain economy of scale, which is one of the benefits of being a big business, eg discounts for bulk-buying.

Partnerships are usually small to medium-sized businesses. Each partner brings a share of capital to the business when it is starting up.

The advantages of a partnership are:

- Workload, responsibility and decision making can be shared amongst the partners – it isn't down to one person.

- Different partners often bring different experiences and skills.

- Finance can be raised more easily compared to a sole trader.

- Customers and suppliers might see a partnership as being less of a risk to deal with compared to a sole trader.

The disadvantages of a partnership are:

- Any profit that the business makes is split between partners.

- Unlimited liability for each partner.

- Arguments between partners might happen and could slow down decision making.

- A legal document known as a partnership agreement needs to be created. The partnership agreement sets out how profits will be split.

Private Limited Companies usually have the letters 'Ltd' after their name but not always so recognising one can sometimes be difficult. A more common type of Limited Company is a Public Limited Company (or 'PLC') but because this is a larger business, we won't learn about it until Higher.

To be an owner of a Ltd company you have to buy shares. These shares are not available to just anyone and normally you would be invited to buy them from people who are already connected to the business, such as family or friends. Normally shareholders would receive a return on the money they have invested in the business called a **dividend**. Even though shareholders own it, the responsibility for running the business is delegated (which simply means given to) a Board of Directors who have the job of managing the company.

When a Ltd company is being set up, legal documents have to be created and sent to an organisation called **Companies House**, where a copy is kept. These documents are called a **Memorandum of Association** and **Articles of Association** and contain detailed information about how the business will operate.

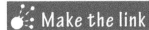

Make the link

Different sources of finance are available to different types of businesses. You will learn about these in Chapter 7, which is on Finance.

The advantages of a Ltd company are:

- Limited liability for shareholders – unlike sole traders and partnerships, if the business fails, shareholders only lose the money they have invested into the company when buying shares. Their own personal possessions (eg a house) would not be sold to pay off the business debts.

- Finance can be raised by selling more shares to existing shareholders or inviting new people to buy.

- Shareholders and Directors can bring different experience and skills.

The disadvantages of a Ltd company are:

- More complicated to set up compared to a sole trader or partnership because of the legal process involved.

- The rules laid down by the law – The Companies Act – have to be followed.

- Each year, financial accounts showing the financial position of the company have to be published.

- The cost of setting up a Ltd company can be high.

GO! Activity

Andy wants to set up his own business. He has a few ideas but doesn't know much about what type of business would be best... should he work himself? Should he have a partner? Does he need to have shareholders? Where does he get money to start-up? Why?

In pairs or in a small group, you have been asked to give Andy some advice.

Recommend, with reasons, a suitable type of business for Andy. Try to explain your advice as clearly as you can - he isn't very business wise!

You could create a factsheet, wiki or even use quick response (QR) codes to display your advice.

Skills

- Communication
- Thinking
- Decision making
- ICT

The public sector

Public sector organisations are owned by the government on behalf of the taxpayer and aim to provide a service to the general public. They are funded by taxes that individuals and businesses have to pay. Different types of taxes exist including income tax, road tax and council tax.

The UK parliament has overall responsibility for what happens in the UK. It is made up of Members of Parliament (MPs), who are elected by the public.

The Scottish Government has delegated responsibility for issues such as education, health and transport. It is run by Members of the Scottish Parliament (MSPs), who are also elected by the public.

Local government organisations (or local authorities) get funding from the Scottish government to deliver specific services in a specific area of Scotland. These include running schools, providing leisure facilities and emptying our bins!

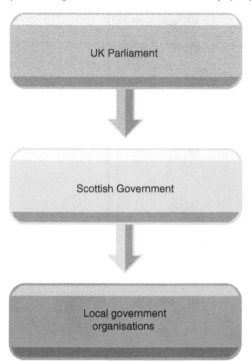

Levels of government

The Scottish Parliament building, Edinburgh

Local government organisations

There are 32 local authorities in Scotland and each has to report to the Scottish government. Each local authority has a council that is made up of local councillors who have been voted in by people living in the local area.

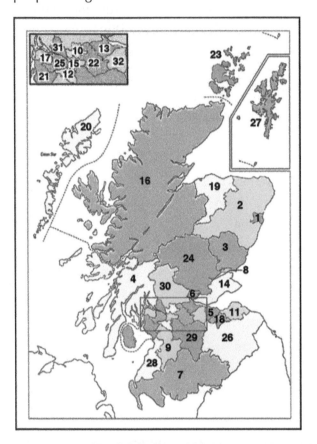

Make the link

How the government affects us as citizens is explored in depth in Economics and Modern Studies.

- Research
- ICT

🔘 Activity

The Scottish Government's website provides a link to each local authority website. Using this information, find out the answers to the following questions. Write these down in your learning journal.

1. Which local authority do you live in?
2. How many people live in your local authority area?
3. Who is the leader of your local authority?
4. How many councillors does your local authority have?
5. Where is the main office of your local authority based?

Third sector

Non-profit making organisations such as charities and voluntary organisations are set up to support specific causes. Charities are regulated by the government and the income they make is put towards a specific cause. For example, The RSPCA uses the income they make to prevent animal cruelty and to promote animal welfare. Voluntary organisations such as community football clubs or youth clubs aim to provide a service to people, but without a profit-making motive.

Social enterprises have a main social or environmental aim rather than to make profit for owners or shareholders but they are run in a business-like way. People know what social enterprises try to do and who they are trying to help. At least half of the profit that social enterprises make, through selling goods and services, must be invested into meeting the stated aim of the social enterprise. Unlike some charities, they don't rely on grants and donations but some social enterprises do become charities. The main difference between a social enterprise and a charity is its legal structure and the fact that social enterprises are less regulated by the government.

Examples of social enterprises

- **The Wise Group**: based in Glasgow, with the aim of helping people into work, improving communities and making life better for people generally.

- **Wooden Spoon Catering**: based in Dundee, with the aim of providing job and education opportunities for women who might be isolated or in a vulnerable position.

- **Ness Soap**: based in Inverness, with the aim of providing opportunities for people to gain work-related skills and gain employment.

⊙ Activity

Further information on social enterprises can be found at:
- Social Enterprise Scotland
- Just Enterprise
- Social Enterprise UK

- Research
- ICT

GO! Activity

Choose a social enterprise in your local area and find out:

- The name of the social enterprise.
- The aim(s) of the social enterprise.
- What products it sells.
- One other interesting piece of information about the social enterprise.

Using the information you have gathered, contribute to the discussion forum that your teacher/lecturer has set up for your class. As well as being able to present findings about your social enterprise, you can read about social enterprises other people in your class have researched.

In your learning journal, write a short paragraph about a social enterprise you have learned about. What is it that interests you about this social enterprise? How much of an impact does it have? Do you have any ideas on what it could do to improve?

Skills

- Research
- ICT
- Decision making
- Thinking

GO! Activity

Create a map of your local high street or shopping centre showing the different businesses available. On your map make sure you include the following pieces of information about each business:

- Its name
- Whether it provides a good or a service
- Sector of industry
- Sector of the economy
- Type of business

To help you create your map, use an online mapping program such as Google Maps or, if you can, use the maps app on a smartphone or tablet computer.

In your learning journal, write a short paragraph about your local high street or shopping centre. How popular is it? Is it an attractive place to visit? What encourages you or puts you off visiting? What could be better?

Skills

- Research
- ICT
- Decision making
- Communication
- Thinking

? Questions

1. Name the three sectors of the economy.
2. Describe two types of business within the private sector.
3. Compare the ownership and control of a sole trader with a Private Limited Company.
4. Suggest a reason why a disagreement between partners of a partnership might slow down decision-making.
5. Describe two advantages of a Private Limited Company.
6. Who is a local government organisation accountable to?
7. Identify two services provided by a local government organisation.
8. What is a social enterprise?
9. Describe a difference between a charity and a social enterprise.
10. Name two methods of funding a social enterprise does not rely on.

Customer satisfaction

Customers are very important to a business because they give the business money in return for receiving a good or a service. Every business has to make sure their customers are as happy as possible. They can try to do this by:

- **Providing the highest possible quality product:** this is covered in more depth in Chapter 5 (Operations).

- **Making sure employees are trained** to the highest level and are knowledgeable about the products on sale. This is covered in more depth on pages 110–112.

- **Having a customer care strategy**: this lets customers know about the level of service that will be provided and, if they make a complaint, how it will be dealt with.

- **Having a customer complaints procedure**: this is a process that the customer and business follows if a customer is unhappy and makes a complaint. It aims to make sure customer complaints are handled in the best way possible.

- **Having an after-sales service**: this gives customers the opportunity to ask questions about their purchase after it has been bought.

Having satisfied customers will encourage them to be loyal to the business, which means they return in the future and make more purchases. It gives the business a good reputation and will help to maximise sales and profit. It can help to increase its share of the market (the number of customers it has).

Activity

Think about a good and bad experience you have had when buying a product.

- What made the experience good or bad?
- What did the business do about it?
- How did the experience make you feel?
- What would have made your experience better?

Share your experience with the rest of your class and record your experience in your learning journal.

Objectives

An **objective** is something a business aims for – it's a target or goal to be achieved.

Objectives help a business to focus on what it is doing and the activities it is doing to achieve its goals.

For example, you have the objective to pass National 5 Business Management but this won't happen by itself – you have to attend classes, participate in activities, complete homework and do extra reading. A business is very similar, eg it won't make a profit without having a list of things it has to do to make the profit.

We have to learn about seven objectives.

Objective	Meaning
Survival	This means to continue trading and it is often the first objective a business has. Survival is important because the other objectives would be pointless if the business didn't survive.
Profit	This means to have more income than costs. It is the main objective of any business in the private sector. Profit is calculated by taking the total income a business has, eg through sales, and subtracting all of the costs it incurs. For example, if the total income of business X was £10,000 and its costs were £4,000, it would make a profit of £6,000.
Provision of a service	This means to provide people with a service that they want. For example, a local government organisation might aim to provide a high quality education service to young people.
Customer satisfaction	This means to make customers happy and to encourage them to make repeat purchases. Customer satisfaction was covered on page 27.
Enterprise	This means to combine resources to produce a product that customers want. It might involve a business developing a new idea and trying to satisfy the wants of customers in a different way – maybe by providing a product that hasn't existed before.

Objective	Meaning
Social responsibility	This means to be seen in a positive way by not harming the local environment or community. For example, a business might invest money into a recycling scheme or only use materials that are not harmful to the environment.
Market share	This can mean two things: • To increase market share. • To become the market leader. If the business aims to increase its market share, this means it wants to increase the number of customers it has. If it has more customers than its competitors (other businesses doing the same thing) it is known as the market leader.

(GO!) Activity

The following table has a list of objectives. Complete tasks 1 and 2.

Task 1
Copy the table out and then tick which objectives different sectors of the economy would have.

	Private	Public	Third
Survival			
Profit			
Provision of a service			
Customer satisfaction			
Enterprise			
Social responsibility			
Market share			

Task 2
Using the information from Task 1 create a mind map, including a description of each objective and at least one reason why each objective is important. If you can, you could also include an example of a business that has that objective.

⚠ Watch point

It is important you remember what each objective actually means as well as why it is important.

Make the link

Different types of business organisations can have similar and also different objectives. The different objectives listed above are explored in more detail throughout this course.

• Thinking
• Decision making

❓Questions

1. What is a customer care strategy?
2. Suggest two reasons why customer service is important.
3. What does 'survival' mean?
4. How do you calculate profit?
5. Why is customer satisfaction important?
6. What information is required to calculate market share?
7. What is social responsibility?
8. What does the term 'market leader' mean?

🔍 Case study

LC Personal Training, Glasgow

LC PT

LC Personal Training was started in July 2020 by Lee Coutts in Glasgow. Lee provides personal fitness training to people of all backgrounds and ages, on a one-to-one basis in a gym and can also provide fitness advice to people online.

Lee always loved his time in the gym, the things that he learned from fitness and the benefits that it brought. He is motivated by seeing people grow in confidence and achieving their fitness goals, so in July 2020 he started his own business. Even though there were a number of risks, Lee believed it was worth it.

Lee started his business with nothing but money being paid out but after a short time, hard work, long hours and dedication, it started to pay off. Some days were better than others, but Lee was in it for the long term and focused on the longer-term rewards rather than the short-term hurdles. He believes that providing a consistent high quality service is important and that achieving customer satisfaction is crucial.

❓Questions

1. What type of business is LC Personal Training?
2. Who owns and runs LC Personal Training?
3. Does Lee provide a product or a service? Justify your choice.
4. What sector of industry does LC Personal Training belong to?
5. Apply the four factors of production to LC Personal Training.
6. Identify two reasons for Lee starting his own business.
7. Suggest a risk Lee faced when starting his business. Justify your choice.
8. From the case study, identify one thing Lee has done to reduce risk.
9. Lee has a number of skills and qualities. From the case study, identify two of these.

10. Why is each skill and quality given in question 9 important to the success of Lee's business?

11. What would have been Lee's first business objective? Give a reason for your answer from the case study.

12. Lee believes customer satisfaction is important. What does this mean?

13. Suggest two reasons why customer satisfaction is important to Lee's business.

14. Would profit be an objective for Lee? Justify your answer.

★ Key questions

1. Outline the role of business in society. In your answer you should refer to:

   - Needs and wants
   - Goods and services
   - Factors of production
   - The importance of enterprise

2. Identify and describe the three sectors of the economy.

3. Describe a type of business in each sector of the economy.

4. Suggest an objective for each type of business given in question 3.

Summary

This chapter provided you with an overview of the role, activities and objectives of business and different types of business organisations.

The learning intentions for this chapter were:

- The role of business
- Types of business organisations
- Customer satisfaction
- Objectives

By successfully answering the key questions, you will have proved that you have grasped the main topics covered in this chapter.

3 Business influences

You should already be able to

- Identify the internal and external stakeholders of a small business.
- Describe the influence stakeholders can have on a small business.
- Describe the external influences that affect small businesses and the impact that these can have.
- Describe a response to the influences on a small business.

What you will learn in this chapter

- External factors
- Internal factors
- Stakeholders

Influences on business: external factors

> **⚠ Watch point**
> Exam questions often ask candidates to explain the impact of external factors.

There are a number of things that can impact on how a business operates. These things can be grouped into two categories:

- **External factors:** these are things outside the control of a business that impact on how it operates.

- **Internal factors:** these are things within a business that impact on how it operates.

External factors

External factors are often referred to as PESTEC factors. PESTEC stands for:

> **⚠ Watch point**
> PESTEC is a useful acronym for remembering different types of external influences.

- Political
- Economic
- Social
- Technological
- Environmental
- Competitive

Political influences

Political influences come from the actions of the government. In Chapter 2, we explored the different levels of government in the United Kingdom.

Government at each level has different powers that can influence how a business behaves.

The UK parliament can introduce a new law that could stop a business from doing something or make them do something in a different way. For example, a new law might require businesses to carry out new health and safety training or to provide certain facilities to its staff.

The UK parliament can also change the amount of tax that individuals and businesses have to pay. The current rate of Value Added Tax (VAT) that customers pay on most goods and services is 20%.

The Scottish government can also introduce certain new laws and has a range of powers in the areas of health, education, transport and housing. For example, Scottish-based students are lucky that they get further and higher education for free – students in England usually have to pay thousands of pounds for a college or university education.

Local government organisations have certain responsibilities for the area they are based in, for example they can grant and refuse planning permission to build a new factory, shop or office. They also have responsibility for environmental health, recreation and local education services.

Economic influences

Economic influence refers to anything that encourages people to spend or not spend money. Some examples include:

Levels of employment: when unemployment is high (lots of people are out of a job), people are more careful about what they spend their money on. They might choose to spend their money on cheaper essential goods rather than more expensive luxurious ones.

Recession: when the amount of money being spent on goods and services gets low and the quantity of products being sold decreases, a country might be 'in recession'. Recession can be one of the reasons why unemployment rates become high. People become much more careful about what they are spending their money on and businesses can often feel the impact of this; their sales and profits might decline.

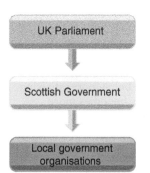

Levels of UK government

Make the link

Politics can be studied as a subject or within Modern Studies. Government policies are explored in more depth in Economics.

Activity

Your teacher/lecturer will show you a list of planning applications that have been made to your local council. You should 'thought shower' as a class the impact that refusing or granting each application might have on:

- People who live and work in the area.
- Businesses that operate in the area.

Remember, the impacts can be positive and negative.

In your learning journal, write about a planning application that is having, or has had, an impact on you. Does it worry you? Why? Why not?

- Thinking
- Decision making

Some people use job centres to try and find work

Make the link

Between economic influences and the impact on our spending behaviour; satisfying our needs becomes more important than spending money on luxury wants.

Make the link

You can study Economics to find out more about these influences.

Skills

- Research
- ICT
- Communication
- Thinking

Fashion is a fast-changing social influence

Interest rates: this is the amount charged by the Bank of England to use money. When the interest rate is low, it is cheaper to borrow money from a bank than when the rate is high. Low interest rates encourage people to borrow money and to spend it, whereas high interest rates encourage people to save their money rather than spend it.

GO! Activity

Choose an economic influence and investigate the impact it can have on individuals and businesses in your local area. Your findings might be presented as:

- A wiki
- A poster
- A PowerPoint presentation

Once you have finished this task, be prepared to present your findings to your class. Your class will judge how useful each presentation is and will give you feedback on:

- **The content:** how much detailed information you provide and the detail you put in about the impact it has.
- **The quality of the presentation:** does it look professional?, is it informative?, has it been put together well?
- **The level of teamwork displayed:** you should make sure each member of the group participates and has a role to play.

You should write down in your learning journal how you think this task went; What went well? What didn't? How would you rate your contribution? What leadership and employability skills did you use?

Social influences

Social influences are those that are concerned with changing opinions, values and people's beliefs.

What people want can change very quickly; for example, their taste in clothing can change rapidly and businesses have to try and keep up (by doing research) on what consumers want. People can be influenced by what they read in the media and by the actions of others, such as celebrities.

Another example of a social influence is the growing number of working practices that are being offered by businesses to their employees. This is often in response to people juggling their work/life balance. Businesses have responded by offering a number of different ways people can work rather than the traditional 9am–5pm job.

Technological influences

Technology is changing very rapidly and has a huge impact on business. More and more people are using technology to communicate with each other and to do business. Some recent technological developments include:

Make the link

Working practices are explored in Chapter 6 (People in business).

Tablet computers	These are keyboard-less computers that let the user do most of the tasks a standard computer or laptop would perform. The use of applications (apps) to allow people to do business and communicate with each other is very popular on these devices, as they are on mobile phones.
Wireless technology	This means using technology without wires and while on the move. Many public transport operators provide wireless access to the internet for their passengers.
Web 2.0	This technology allows people to interact with each other, eg via social networking sites, blogs and wikis. It is popular with businesses for advertising their products and for communicating with customers. Social media tools such as Facebook, Twitter and Instagram are popular examples.
Cloud computing	This is becoming popular in managing business information. Information is stored on the internet – in the cloud – and often means cheaper IT and staffing costs for a business.

Tablet computers are a recent form of portable technology

Activity

Make a list of the different ways new technologies can impact upon a business. Try to think about the use of social media, smart phones and cloud-based computing systems. Be prepared to discuss these in small groups and with the rest of your class.

- Thinking
- Decision making

Environmental influences

The weather is an example of an environmental influence. When it is hot some businesses do better and when it is cold other businesses do better.

When it is hot, businesses like ice cream vans do better – nobody wants an ice cream when it is cold! Businesses that sell more in hot weather include:	When it is cold, a clothes shop sells more warm clothes than an ice cream seller will sell ice creams! Businesses that sell more in cold weather include:
• Ice cream sellers • Shorts and t-shirt suppliers • Outdoor swimming pools	• Suppliers of heaters and heating • Warm clothing suppliers • Warm food suppliers (eg hot soup)

Make the link

Being socially responsible is often an aim of a business in response to different environmental factors.

Businesses are becoming more aware of the need to be environmentally friendly and sustainable (in response to having to be more socially responsible) and have taken a lot of steps to:

- Increase the recycling of waste products (eg by providing different colour bins for recycling different products).

- Reduce their carbon footprint (eg by encouraging transport sharing and considering ways to reduce the need to travel).

- Increase use of environmentally-friendly products.

- Decrease pollution (eg noise, lighting, traffic, chemicals).

Competitive influences

A competitor is another business offering the same or a similar product to your business. Businesses don't like competition because they can take away customers and profits. However, competition has benefits for customers:

- More choice of where to purchase.

- Goods might be priced cheaper.

- More special offers might be given.

- The service offered is often of a higher quality.

Two shops selling the same goods have to compete for customers

Case study

Simpsons Garden Centre, Inverness

Simpsons Garden Centre is based in Inverness. It has the aim of reducing its impact on the environment. Simpsons Garden Centre has put the following measures in place.

- They have a written environmental policy.

- They recycle whenever they can.

- Staff are trained in environmental issues.

- Products are sourced locally, where possible, to cut down on traffic pollution.

- Water wastage is reduced by only watering plants by hand.

- Movement sensors are used to switch on lights only when necessary.

- They heat the restaurant by recycling heat from the restaurant's kitchen.

? Questions

1. Suggest a reason why Simpsons Garden Centre is committed to the environment.
2. Suggest a reason why staff are trained in environmental issues.
3. Why does using movement sensors cut down on electricity usage?
4. Why does sourcing local products cut down on pollution?
5. Why do they water plants by hand?

GO! Activity

With a partner, have a discussion about your local shopping centre or retail park.

- Make a list of businesses that are in competition with each other.
- What are the benefits of competition for you as a customer?

Write down your answers in your learning journal.

- Thinking
- Communication

? Questions

1. A list of external influences is given below. Name the type of influence that each one is.

   - Refusing to grant planning permission to build a new shop.
   - People wanting to buy brightly-coloured and decorative wellington boots rather than dark green ones.
   - The introduction of a new type of computer.
   - The opening of a takeaway shop next to a fast food restaurant.
   - The increase of a tax rate.
   - The number of people out of work rising.
   - Changing weather.
   - Encouraging people to reuse towels in a hotel rather than using clean ones every day.
   - Increase in people wanting to have flexible working arrangements.

2. Name the three levels of government in the UK.
3. Give two ways the UK parliament could influence a business.
4. What is a recession?
5. Does a business benefit when interest rates are low or high? Why?
6. How do businesses try to keep up with changing tastes and fashion?
7. Web 2.0 is used often for what purpose?
8. Name three ways a business can be environmentally friendly.
9. What is a competitor?
10. Suggest three benefits of competition for a consumer.

Influences on business: internal factors

We can group the main internal factors into three groups:

- **Financial**: the availability or lack of finance.

- **Human resources**: the employees and managers within the business.

- **Current technology**: technology being used by the business at the present time.

Financial influences

A business might be affected internally by a lack of finance (money). Consider the following example:

Joe is a window cleaner based in a small village outside Glasgow. He wants to expand his business so that he can clean the windows of houses in Glasgow. However, he has a problem – he doesn't have the money to buy a van to be able to transport his ladder and other materials.

The example above shows how a business can be affected by a lack of finance; in this example, the aim of growth cannot be achieved by Joe as he doesn't have enough money to grow his business.

Businesses might be forced to make decisions based on the availability of finance. A lack of finance might mean that:

- A machine cannot be bought.
- Staff cannot be paid or more staff employed.
- An advertising campaign can't be carried out.
- Loans have to be obtained from a bank.
- Raw materials to be used in production cannot be paid for.

Human resource influences

People who work for a business are known as the workforce or human resource. Employees are paid by a business to carry out a number of tasks related to the job that they perform.

- **Cleaners** are employed to, for instance, clean offices and shops.
- **Administrative Assistants** may be employed to type letters and send out business documents.
- **Doctors** are employed to make people feel better by giving medicines and treating medical problems.

Employees can affect how a business works by making decisions, carrying out their work to a poor standard and also by taking industrial action. Staff who are poorly trained might not have the skills to perform their jobs well.

Managers are promoted employees who are paid extra money in return for extra responsibilities. They have more decision-making powers than employees but in turn this brings a higher risk of something going wrong.

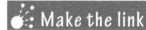

Make the link

Finance is explored in more depth in Chapter 7.

Make the link

Chapter 6 features a more in-depth discussion of human resources.

Current technology

The technology that a business has (at the present time) can influence how the business operates. If the technology is out of date, this might mean that orders can't be processed as quickly as possible or things can go wrong, eg machines can break down.

Businesses who invest lots of money into new technology can often have a competitive edge over their competitors.

Stakeholders

A stakeholder is a person or a group of people who have an interest in the success of a business. Stakeholders have an **interest** in a business and can **influence** it in different ways. Some of the ways stakeholders can influence a business have already been explored (eg internal influences), but we need to look at this in more detail.

⚡ Make the link

Technology is explored in more depth throughout this book, including earlier in this chapter.

Stakeholder	Interest	Influence
Owners These are the people who have started the business.	• Want the business to make profit. • Want a good return on the money they have invested.	• Can invest more or less capital in the business. • Make decisions.
Shareholders These are the people who have bought shares in a Limited Company.	• Want the business to make profit. • Want a good return on the money they have invested in the form of dividends.	• Can invest more or less capital into the business. • Can make decisions by voting at Annual General Meetings.
Employees These are the people who work for a business – the human resource.	• Want to receive a good rate of pay. • Want to be treated fairly. • Want good working conditions. • Want to receive continuing professional development and training. • Want to receive as many benefits as possible, eg company car.	• Can take industrial action such as a strike. • Can make products of a poor quality.
Banks These are organisations that provide businesses with financial services.	• Want the business to open a bank account. • Want loans to be repaid on time. • Want mortgages on premises to be taken out and repaid on time.	• Can refuse to provide loans. • Can demand repayment of loans instantly. • Can charge high interest rates on loans.
Customers These are the people who buy goods and services from a business.	• Want a good quality product. • Want to pay a reasonable price for the product being bought. • Want to receive good customer service.	• Can shop elsewhere. • Through word-of-mouth or online reviews can provide positive or negative feedback to others.

Suppliers These are organisations that provide raw materials to a business.	• Want to be paid on time for the materials provided. • Want to receive repeat orders for materials.	• Can increase the price they charge. • Can refuse to provide credit on materials. • May not deliver on time.
Local community This is a group of people who live near to an organisation.	• Want jobs in the local area. • Want businesses in the local area to be socially responsible.	• Can make complaints to their local council or MP. • Can protest, eg by writing to the local newspaper.
Pressure groups These are organisations that try to influence other organisations.	• Support and promote a specific interest or cause.	• Can hold demonstrations and protests to raise awareness of an issue.
Local government This government organisation has responsibility for specific things within a certain area.	• Want jobs in the local area. • Want businesses to invest money into the local area.	• Can refuse or grant planning permission. • Can close down businesses that do not comply with environmental health requirements (eg restaurants).
National government This government organisation has overall responsibility for what happens in the UK.	• Want low unemployment figures so that less money is paid out on benefits. • Want taxes to be paid so that money can be invested into other parts of the economy. • Want the law to be followed.	• Can change the amount of tax to be paid. • Can introduce or change the law.

? Questions

1. What is a stakeholder?
2. Give three examples of a stakeholder.
3. Label the following interests with the correct stakeholder:

   - Wants training on doing a task.
   - Wants to receive payment for supplying flour to a baker.
   - Wants them to open another account for saving money.
   - Wants extra jobs in the country so that less money is paid out in benefits.
   - Wants the testing of medicine on animals to be stopped.
   - Wants the nearby airport to stop allowing planes to take off during the night so that they can get a good night's sleep.
   - Wants longer to be able to return items to the shop where they have been purchased.

GO! Activity

Create a mind map showing the interest and influence of different stakeholders for a local business of your choice. Try to include at least three stakeholders. You can do this task on paper or using online mind-mapping software.

- Thinking
- Decision making

4. Label the following influences with the correct stakeholder:

- Complained to the local council about pollution from a nearby factory.
- Bought more shares in a company.
- Decided to use a different hotel on a business trip because they received poor service on a previous visit.
- Decided not to allow a business to build an extension onto their existing shop.
- Visited their MP because they are unhappy with the volume of traffic on the road outside their house.
- Decided to increase the amount of money to be repaid on a loan.
- Decided to request immediate payment of a recent bill for raw materials.

★ Key questions

1. Describe the difference between external and internal influences.
2. Outline how three external factors can impact upon a business.
3. Give an example of how the following can influence a business decision:

- Finance
- Human resources
- Current technology

4. For each of the following stakeholders, suggest an interest and influence for each one in a business:

- Employees
- Customers
- Suppliers
- The government

Summary

This chapter provided you with an overview of the different factors and people that can influence how a business operates.

The learning intentions for this chapter were:

- External factors

- Internal factors

- Stakeholders

By successfully answering the key questions, you will have proved that you have grasped the main topics covered in this chapter.

1 END OF UNIT MATERIAL

Unit assessment

If you are required to do the unit assessment, you need to show your teacher that you have met the learning outcomes and assessment standards for each unit. To do this, your teacher might get you to undertake some tasks at the end of the unit or might get you to gather evidence as you complete the unit. There are a large number of ways that you can show you have met the evidence requirements of the unit and this can vary from unit to unit. The following list gives you an idea of what you might be asked to do.

- Quiz with multiple-choice questions

- Extended-response questions

- An oral presentation

- A mini research project

- A mini project involving creating a blog or wiki

- An information sheet

- A portfolio

ASSESSMENT INFO

To pass the unit assessment, you have to achieve each assessment standard. For this unit, the learning outcomes and assessment standards are:

Outcome 1: Give an account of the key objectives and activities of small and medium-sized business organisations by:

- Outlining the role of business organisations in society.

- Outlining why customer satisfaction is crucial to the success of a business organisation.

- Outlining the objectives of business organisations in different sectors of the economy.

Outcome 2: Apply knowledge and understanding of factors that impact on the activities of small and medium-sized business organisations by:

- Outlining how internal factors impact on business activity.

- Outlining how external factors impact on business activity.

- Examining the impact stakeholders have on business activity.

Your teacher will make sure you know what you have to do to pass each unit. Remember, not everyone will be required to do the unit assessment.

> ⚠ **Watch point**
>
> The outcomes and assessment standards give you an indication of the things that will come up in your unit assessment.

Exam questions: Understanding Business

- Describe the advantages and disadvantages of a partnership. (4 marks)

Make sure you read the question carefully as every word is there for a reason. It is good practice to break the question down into parts before you start to answer it – this will help to make sure you answer it the best you can.

Describe the advantages and disadvantages of a partnership. (4 marks)

| The command word – your instruction on how to answer the question. | You must give advantages and disadvantages to get full marks. | Only a partnership – no other type of business. |

Sample answer

The advantages of a partnership are that the workload is shared amongst partners **(1 mark)** and different partners bring different skills to the business **(1 mark)**. The disadvantages are that any profit has to be split **(1 mark)** and each partner has unlimited liability **(1 mark)**.

Examiner's commentary

The candidate has clearly answered the question by giving two correct advantages and two correct disadvantages. They could also have given three advantages and one disadvantage for full marks because the question didn't specify a minimum number of each that had to be given. However, before full marks can be awarded at least one of each would have to be given. The answer is clearly written. **(4/4)**

- Describe the impact external factors can have on a business. (3 marks)
- Compare the objectives of a private sector and public sector organisation. (3 marks)
- Outline the importance of customer satisfaction to a business. (3 marks)
- Describe the factors of production. (4 marks)
- Identify and describe the sectors of industry. (6 marks)
- Outline the interests of three stakeholders in a business. (3 marks)

Check your progress

	HELP NEEDED	GETTING THERE	CONFIDENT
The role of business in society	◯	◯	◯
Needs and wants	◯	◯	◯
Goods and services	◯	◯	◯
The business cycle	◯	◯	◯
Factors of production	◯	◯	◯
Wealth creation	◯	◯	◯
Sectors of industry	◯	◯	◯
Sectors of the economy: private, public and third	◯	◯	◯
Sole traders	◯	◯	◯
Partnerships	◯	◯	◯
Private Limited Companies	◯	◯	◯
National government organisations	◯	◯	◯
Local government organisations	◯	◯	◯
Non-profit making organisations	◯	◯	◯
Social enterprises	◯	◯	◯
Customer satisfaction	◯	◯	◯

	HELP NEEDED	GETTING THERE	CONFIDENT
Objectives	◯	◯	◯
Internal influences	◯	◯	◯
External influences (PESTEC)	◯	◯	◯
Stakeholders	◯	◯	◯

What actions do you need to take to improve your knowledge?

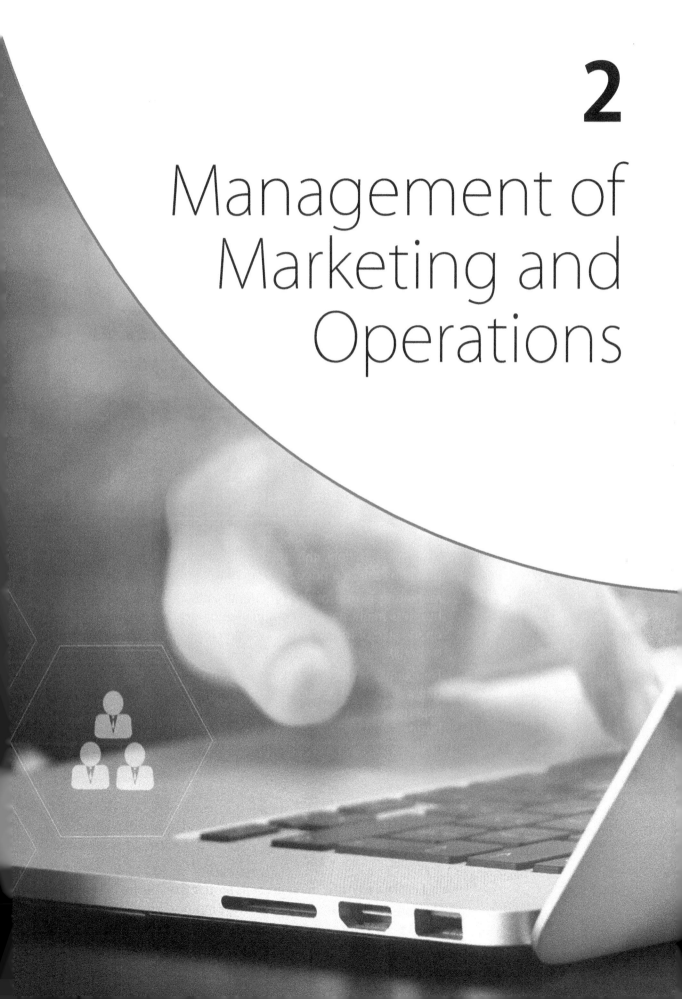

2

Management of Marketing and Operations

4 Management of Marketing

What is marketing?

Marketing involves trying to meet the needs and wants of customers. It does this by finding out what they want and providing this at a price that can make a profit.

Marketing is one of the functional activities of a business. A business might have its own marketing department, depending on the size of the business, or marketing might be done by the owner(s).

For example, in a Private Limited Company marketing activities might be carried out by a separate department that has experience in this area. However, in a smaller, sole-trader business, the sole trader might carry out marketing activities as well as everything else.

Markets

Goods and services are supplied to customers in a market. A market is where customers (the buyer) and sellers (the supplier) come together. A market can exist in a number of places, for example:

- **On a website:** the seller sells products online for customers to buy (eg Tesco online shopping or eBay). This is often referred to as **e-commerce** or **e-business**.

- **In a shop:** the seller has products on shelves for customers to look at and buy (eg in a newsagents).

- **Over the telephone:** the seller might telephone a customer to encourage them to buy something (eg double glazing).

- **Through an internet-enabled telephone or tablet computer:** the seller might have an application (an app) that customers can access, search for a product and then buy it (eg Dominos pizza or Odeon cinema tickets).

You can shop online for a wide variety of goods

Why is marketing important?

Marketing is an important activity because it:

- Can attract new customers by letting them know about the range of products the business has.

- It can allow the business to enter new markets (eg using the internet to sell a product on the other side of the world).

- It can help the business grow by entering new markets.

- Can increase the amount of profit a business makes.

Make the link

Marketing can help a business achieve a number of its objectives, eg to make a profit and to increase market share.

The role of marketing

Marketing can help a business increase the number of customers buying from the business **(market growth)**. This will help them to increase the proportion of customers it has from the whole market **(market share)**, and if they have the most customers compared to other businesses in the same market, they can become **market leader**.

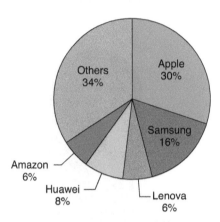

The chart shows that Apple has the largest market share of tablet computers (although there are lots of smaller companies that in total occupy a larger share of the market). The chart shows that Apple has a share of the market that is double in size compared to Samsung.

Surveys can be useful sources of information

Customers and market segments

Customers are important stakeholders as they buy goods and services from a business. Businesses often focus their product towards a specific group of people. This is known as their **target market** or **market segment**. They do this for a number of reasons:

Reason	Why is it important?
To make sure the product is suitable and specific to the needs of the customer group.	The product will not sell if it is not what the customer wants nor meets their requirements.
To make sure that the product is sold in the most suitable place where the customer can access it.	The product will not sell if the customer is unable to purchase it in a place convenient to them.
So that a price can be set that will reflect the market segment.	Higher prices can be charged for products that are seen to be of a higher quality and therefore the business would make more profit.
To make sure advertising and promotion campaigns are targeted towards the correct customer group.	Money would be wasted on promoting products to the wrong market segment and no sales would be made.

The market can be segmented in a number of ways with each segment having a common characteristic.

Segment	What it is	Example
Gender	Segmenting by gender means to market a product towards a specific gender, eg male or female.	A perfume could be designed in two variations: one for men and one for women.
Age	Segmenting by age means to market a product towards people of a certain age group.	A holiday could be designed for people who are 18–30 years old.
Occupation	Segmenting by occupation means to market a product towards people who do a particular job.	A stethoscope is designed for doctors, nurses and other healthcare professionals.
Religious or cultural belief	Segmenting by religious or cultural belief means to market a product towards people who follow a specific religious or cultural faith.	Halal meat for people who are Muslim.
Income/social class	Segmenting by income or social class means to market a product towards people who have a certain level of income or belong to a particular social group (eg working class or upper class).	Supermarket own brands, eg Tesco Value brand, is aimed at people with a low income whereas Tesco Finest is aimed at people with a higher income.
Geographical location	Segmenting by geographical location means to market a product towards people who live in a particular location.	The climate and temperature in a country will determine the type of clothing sold, eg warmer clothing for colder countries!
Lifestyle	Segmenting by lifestyle means to market a product towards people who lead a particular life, eg whether they are into sport and fitness.	Lucozade sports drinks are aimed at people taking part in exercise to provide them with energy.

Skills

- Thinking
- Decision making
- ICT

Activity

For each of the following products, name an appropriate market segment.

- Ferrari sports car
- Lynx deodorant
- Pampers nappies
- Football boots
- A treadmill
- First Choice Splash World Holidays
- Nail extensions

Skill

- Decision making

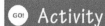

Activity

In a group, choose a product and answer the following questions:

1. What market segment is the product aimed at?
2. How do you know which market segment it is aimed at?
3. How does the business promote and advertise the product?
4. Where is the product sold?
5. Do some research and find out the market share the product has.
6. Using the information found in question 5, create a pie chart (using Excel if you can) showing the product's percentage market share against the other products in the same market.
7. Make a list of ways that the product could increase its market share.

Be prepared to discuss your answers with the rest of the class.

? Questions

1. What is marketing?
2. What is a market?
3. What is provided in a market?
4. Name three places where a market can exist.
5. Can marketing help a business achieve its objectives?
6. How does marketing help to attract customers?
7. How can marketing help a business to grow?
8. Define the term market growth.
9. Define the term market share.
10. Define the term market leader.
11. If one business increases its market share, what will happen to another business at the same time?
12. Define the term market segmentation.
13. Name three ways a market could be segmented.
14. The market for children's toys is segmented by age. What does this mean?
15. The market for running shoes is segmented by lifestyle. What does this mean?

The marketing mix

The marketing mix consists of four elements that help a business to achieve its marketing objectives. The four elements are known as the four 'P's: product, price, place and promotion.

A business needs to have a correct mix of the marketing mix to have successful marketing. Successful marketing needs the correct quantities of each 'P'; it is like baking a cake – you need the correct quantities of each ingredient or the cake doesn't turn out the way that it should!

Element	Description	Why is it important?
Product	This is the actual item (a good or a service) that is produced by the business and then sold in a market.	The product must be what the customer wants or they will not buy it. Market research helps a business to identify what the customer wants.
Price	This is how much money a business charges the customer to buy the product. Different pricing strategies are used to determine the price of a product.	The product must be a price that the customer will buy it at. The price must not be too high compared to competition because customers will buy from them if it is. The price must reflect the quality of the product, but at the same time, allow the business to cover costs and make a profit.
Place	This is the way the business makes the product available to the customer and where the product is sold (the market).	The product must be accessible to the customer (ie they must be able to obtain it). The product might be sold via different places including shops, websites, TV and through smart phone apps.
Promotion	This is how customers are told that the product exists and are encouraged in different ways to buy it. Promotion is more than just advertising.	The product must be promoted and advertised to customers so that they know it exists. Different promotion methods are used to encourage customers to buy a product.

⚠ Watch point

The marketing mix is a popular assessment topic. Each element is considered in more depth in pages 58–76.

🌳 Skills

- Thinking
- Research
- Communication

GO! Activity

In the same groups as the activity on page 54, and using the same product, answer the following questions:

1. What product is being sold?
2. What price is charged for the product?
3. What place(s) is the product sold in?
4. How is the product promoted?
5. What are the costs and benefits of the methods of promotion used?
6. In what way could the marketing of the product be improved? (Try to refer to each element of the marketing mix.)

🔍 Case study

Vincent Barbers, Glasgow

Vincent Barbers in Glasgow offers its male customers the ultimate grooming experience. It provides men with haircuts, massages, shaves and lots of other beauty treatments. As well as providing these, it has a number of products (eg hair wax, shampoo, body wash) that its customers can buy.

Vincent Barbers, based in Glasgow's city centre, is easily accessible to customers by train and road. Customer service is very important and its customers are provided with complimentary drinks and magazines. The prices of its products are available on its website, as are details of special grooming packages at discounted rates.

As well as the website, Vincent Barbers uses social media (eg Facebook) to let customers know about its products.

? Questions

1. Identify and describe the sector of industry Vincent Barbers belongs to.
2. What market segment does Vincent Barbers cater for?
3. Describe two advantages of focusing on a specific market segment.
4. From the case study, identify two services provided by Vincent Barbers.
5. From the case study, identify two goods provided by Vincent Barbers.
6. Suggest two reasons why customer service is important to Vincent Barbers.
7. Identify the place Vincent Barbers is based.
8. From the case study, identify two promotion methods used by Vincent Barbers.

Make the link

Market research obtains a variety of information. The higher quality the information is, the better it will be for decision-making. For this course, you have to undertake research for your coursework assessment.

? Questions

1. What is the marketing mix?
2. Match each element given below to the appropriate 'P'.
   - The way customers are informed that a product exists.
   - The amount of money being charged for the product.
   - Where the customer can buy the product.
   - The good or service being sold.
3. How do businesses make sure they provide a product that a customer wants?
4. For each element of the marketing mix, suggest why it is important.

Make the link

External factors can play a big role in the success or failure of a new product. Try to think about how each external factor would influence product development.

Product

Product development

Before a product is made available to customers in a market, it has to go through development. A number of activities take place during product development.

- Market research is carried out to find out what the customer wants.

- Ideas for the product are generated based on market research information.

- A model of the product might be created – this is known as a **prototype**. This lets people see what the product would look like and how it would work.

- **Test marketing** – where customers get to try out the product and provide feedback – might take place.

- Changes might be made to the product after the prototype has been created based on the feedback it received.

- The method of production has to be decided.

- The price that will be charged for the product has to be decided.

- The place that the product will be sold has to be decided.

- The methods of promotion that will be used have to be decided.

There are lots of risks associated with developing a new product and the importance of product development should not be underestimated. Making sure that the product is developed in the best possible way will make sure it has the best possible chance when it is launched onto the market.

Some of the risks a business faces when it develops a new product are:

- Customers might not want the product (ie there is no demand for it) and therefore not buy it.

- The money invested into developing the product would be wasted and this could put the business into financial difficulty.

- The reputation of the business could be damaged if it produces a product nobody wants or that is of poor quality.

- External factors (eg competition or the economy) might impact upon the success of the product.

Make the link

Other departments in a business (eg finance and operations) will be involved during product development. This is because they have specialist knowledge that will help the marketing department make important decisions.

GO! Activity

You and your partner are the marketing managers of a company. You are about to launch a new and exciting product.

Task 1

You have to decide what product you are going to produce. You are free to choose any product, but the following list might help you to get started:

- A computer game
- A breakfast cereal
- A children's toy
- A chocolate bar
- An energy drink
- A mobile phone application

- Thinking
- Decision making
- ICT
- Enterprise
- Communication

Task 2

Answer the following questions:

- Is your product a good or a service?
- What market segment will the product be aimed at?
- What will the new product be called?
- How will you price the product?
- How will you promote the product?

Task 3

Do some research to find out what would happen before the product is launched (ie what stages of product development it would have to go through). Make a note of these stages.

Task 4

Write down some of the risks associated with the development of your product.

Task 5

Create at least one of the following for your product:

- A drawing showing what the product would look like.
- A poster, webpage or social networking site advertising your new product.
- A piece of packaging for your new product.

Task 6

Once you have finished this task, be prepared to present your findings to your class. Your class will judge your product and will give you feedback on:

- **Content** (eg stages to be carried out during development, risks).
- **Quality of your creation in Task 5** (Does it look professional? Is it informative? Has it been put together well?).
- **The level of teamwork displayed** (you should make sure each member of the group participates).

You should write down in your learning journal how you think these tasks went; What went well? What didn't? How would you rate your contribution? What leadership and employability skills did you use?

Product life cycle

Once a product has been launched onto the market, it has a life cycle. The product life cycle shows the different stages of the product's life.

The four stages are:

- Introduction
- Growth
- Maturity
- Decline

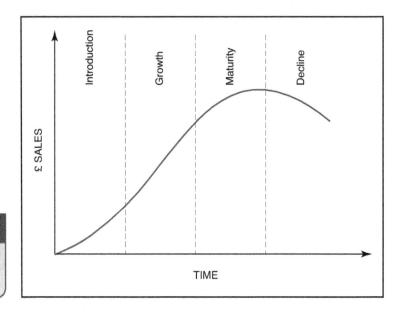

Introduction	Growth	Maturity	Decline
The product is introduced onto the market.	Sales of the product are growing.	Sales of the product reach their highest.	Sales of the product begin to fall.
Lots of advertising and promotion to encourage sales.	Sales are growing because more customers know that it exists as a result of lots of promotion (during introduction).	Because sales are at their highest, this is the most profitable stage.	This is because the product is getting older and newer versions are coming onto the market; customers no longer want it.

Some products have a very long product life cycle whereas others don't. For example, a Mars Bar has a longer product life cycle compared to a mobile phone, which tends goes out of date very quickly.

Branding

We hear the term 'brand' all the time, but what does it actually mean? A brand can be a logo, name or symbol that is given to a group or type of product. Some businesses have their own brands to help separate them from other products. For example, Tesco Value and Tesco Finest.

For example:

	Heinz is an example of a brand – it is a recognisable name.
	McDonald's Golden Arches is an example of a logo that is recognisable – we don't need to see the name McDonald's before we know what product it is.

Businesses have a brand for a number of reasons:

- So that it is recognisable to customers and can act as a marketing and promotion tool. This can help customers to distinguish a business from competitors.

- To encourage customers to become repeat customers – they become 'brand loyal' (this means they stick to buying one particular brand).

- Higher prices can sometimes be charged for branded products because people often associate them with being of a high quality. This can increase profit.

- New products can be introduced to the market easily as the brand name is already well known. For example, Apple can easily introduce a new product (for example, a mobile phone) because the brand name Apple is well known.

GO! Activity

Create a graffiti wall with the names of different products. Use this as a basis for a class discussion on the position of each product on the product life cycle. (Try to choose products that have been around for a long time as well as ones that are newer.) Record what you learned about one product in your learning journal – put a picture of it in too.

- Thinking
- Communication

However, there are some disadvantages to having a brand:

- If a product within the brand is poor or gets a bad reputation (perhaps it isn't environmentally friendly for example), this can damage the reputation of the whole brand name.

- Some people try to copy brands and produce their own fake product. This gives customers the impression that it is a real branded product, but it isn't.

- Establishing a brand is a time consuming, lengthy and expensive process. This might have an impact upon the profitability of the business.

? Questions

1. Name two activities that take place during product development.
2. What is test marketing?
3. Suggest two risks associated with developing a new product.
4. Identify four stages of the product life cycle.
5. At which stage does lots of advertising take place?
6. At which stage is profit highest?
7. At which stage does competition impact upon product sales?
8. What is a brand?
9. Outline two advantages of branding.
10. Outline two disadvantages of branding.

Price

Deciding the price

Deciding how much to charge for a product is not as easy as you might think. A business has to take into account different factors:

- The life cycle of the product.

- The price charged by competitors.

- How much it costs to make the product.

- How much profit is wanted.

- How much of the product can be supplied.

- The market segment that the product is focused towards.

Factor	Explanation
The life cycle of the product	Products at the beginning of the life cycle might be priced higher because they are in demand and they may have incurred high research and development costs. As demand for them begins to fall, the price might be reduced. Products in the decline stage are often reduced in price so that they continue to sell.
The price charged by competitors	The business needs to make sure that their price is not more than competitors as they might lose customers to them.
How much it costs to make the product	A business must cover its costs in order to break-even (see page 126). It will calculate how much it costs to make the product before deciding the price, to make sure that costs are covered.
How much profit is wanted	The more profit that is wanted, the higher the price that will need to be charged. If profit is not the main aim of the business (see page 25), then this will not be as much of a consideration.
How much of the product can be supplied	Products that are not made in large quantities might be priced higher than those that are easily made.
The market segment that the product is focused towards	Products that are aimed at people with high incomes might be priced higher or products that are aimed at people with a low income (eg supermarket own brands) might be priced lower.

Pricing strategies

The price charged depends on the pricing strategy that the business is using.

Name	Description	Reason why it is used
Low price	The price charged is lower than the price charged by competitors. For example: If a competitor is charging £4.00 the business might charge £3.50.	The product will be bought by customers because it is cheaper than competitors.
High price	The price charged is higher than the price charged by competitors. For example: If a competitor is charging £4.00 the business might charge £4.50.	The product will be bought by customers because they think it is of a higher quality than competitors.

Make the link

Between quality and price.

Make the link

Promotional pricing is an example of promotion.

Promotional pricing	The price charged is lower than normal for a short period. For example: The price of the product is normally £10.00 but might be reduced to £6.00 for a short period.	The product will be bought by customers because it is on special offer.
Cost-plus pricing	The cost of making the product is calculated before a % is added on for profit. For example: It costs the business £3 to make the profit and they want to make a profit of 50%. The business will add 50% onto £3 (£1.50) and this will be the selling price. The product would therefore cost £4.50 to the customer.	This method ensures that the cost of making the product is covered and a profit is made.
Psychological pricing	The price charged by the business makes the customer think the product is cheaper than it is. For example: Rather than charging £1.00, 99p is charged.	Customers think that the product is cheaper and therefore buy it. (The product is usually only a couple of pence cheaper than what it would normally have been sold for, eg £1 rather than 99p but it does make a difference in their minds.)

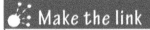

Make the link

How people behave is studied in Psychology.

? Questions

1. Name three factors to be considered when setting a price.
2. Name three pricing strategies.
3. A business must use cost-plus pricing to price a product. Explain how this works.
4. Why must a business work out its break-even point when setting a price?
5. A product's demand is decreasing. What impact will this have on price? Justify your answer.
6. Why is psychological pricing used?

Place

Business location

Businesses have to decide where to locate – this means, where to have their shop or where to sell their product.

A number of things have to be considered when deciding where to locate.

Factor	Why?
Where the customer is	There is no point in setting up a business in a place where there are no customers. Market research will help to identify where customers exist and where the business could locate to meet the needs of these customers.
Availability of suitable premises	The business might need a certain size of shop or a shop with certain facilities (eg a kitchen or large car park). There might only be premises available in certain places.
Parking facilities	Customers need to be able to access the business easily or they might be put off from using the business. It is also important that the business has disabled car parking facilities available.
Suitable infrastructure	Infrastructure refers to the availability of water, gas, electricity and transport links. This is important so that the business can operate (it wouldn't get very far without electricity!) and so that customers, suppliers and other stakeholders can access it.
Government incentives and grants	Sometimes the government will offer incentives (usually a sum of money that doesn't need to be repaid) to encourage businesses to set-up in a specific location or area.
The market segment	Depending on the customer group being targeted, this might influence where the business locates. For example, a shop selling clothing for skiers might open up next to a ski slope.
Employee availability	Employees might be needed to work in the business and therefore employees with suitable skills need to be available nearby.
Competition	A business might want to set up as far away as possible from its competition or it might want to be as close as possible to try and increase their market share.
Environmental impact	Businesses have to consider the environment when deciding on a location. They need to make sure that they are socially responsible when undertaking any construction work and setting up.

GO! Activity

As a class, discuss why different businesses in your area have located where they have. Think about the different factors that have influenced their choice of location.

As an individual or group activity, you might want to draw a map of a local retail park and think about why different businesses have located there.

Write a brief comment in your learning journal about what you have learned about business location.

Skills

- Communication
- Thinking
- Decision making

✦ Make the link

Environmental impact links in with being socially responsible.

GO! Activity

Happy Holidays is a new business looking to open a shop in a retail park in Glasgow. It is considering a number of places but North Glasgow Retail Park seems like a good option. The following picture shows North Glasgow Retail Park.

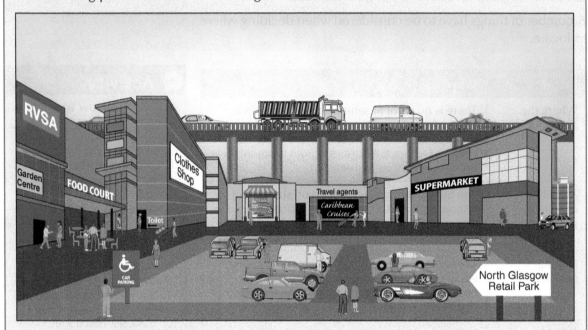

1. Suggest reasons why Happy Holidays would want to locate at North Glasgow Retail Park.
2. For each reason given in question 1, explain why this is important.
3. Are there any other factors Happy Holidays will have to consider before making a final choice of location?

Skills

- Thinking
- Decision making

Distribution methods

A business has to decide how to physically get the product to the customer. This is of course, assuming that the product is a tangible good. Some products might be provided electronically via the internet.

The four main methods of distribution are:

Make the link

Businesses have to consider the environmental impact of each distribution method carefully. They must be seen as socially responsible.

Products might be delivered using the road network.

Advantages	Disadvantages
• Often cheaper than other methods. • Delivery is often quick. • Customer receives the product direct to their door.	• It is difficult to transport large products. • Not as environmentally friendly as other methods. • Roadworks might cause delays.

Products might be delivered by train.

Advantages	Disadvantages
• Large products can be transported. • Large quantities can be transported.	• There isn't a train station in every location or even a rail line. • Not a door-to-door service.

Products might be delivered by aircraft.

Advantages	Disadvantages
• Products can be transported across the world more quickly than by sea. • Large amounts of small products can be transported.	• Large items cannot be transported. • Products need to be taken to an airport to be loaded onto the aircraft – this could be expensive. • Not a door-to-door service.

Products might be delivered by boat.

Advantages	Disadvantages
• Larger products can be transported. • Products can be transported across the world.	• It is time consuming to transport products across the world. • Not a door-to-door service.

? Questions

1. Name three factors to be considered when deciding on a business location.
2. What is infrastructure?
3. Why is employee availability important?
4. The environment needs to be considered when setting up a business. Why?
5. Suggest two advantages of using road transport to distribute products.
6. Suggest two advantages of using air transport to distribute products.
7. Do all products need to be physically transported? Why?

Promotion

Advertising

Advertising makes customers aware that a product exists. It includes information about the product and tries to encourage people to buy it. Advertising is important to increase sales because customers can't buy a product if they don't know it exists.

Internet websites

An **internet website** is a collection of information in one place. It can be accessed by typing a website address into an internet browser (eg Internet Explorer). A website address is known as a URL – Uniform Resource Locator.

Quick Response (QR) codes can also be used to direct people to a business website. A QR code is a barcode. When it is scanned using a tablet computer or smartphone, it takes a person to a website.

A business might have a website to communicate information about its products and also to sell them online; this is called **e-commerce**.

E-commerce has grown quickly over the past few years. Many people now do their shopping online and seek products at cheaper prices online.

Advantages	Disadvantages
• Customers worldwide can be targeted. • Customers can buy online 24/7 from anywhere they want. • Online discounts can be given. • Product information can be updated and accessed quickly. • 3D views of the product can often be seen. • Products can be customised using online software so the customer can see what their product would look like. • Stock availability can be checked instantly. • Businesses don't necessarily have to pay for premises to display stock. • Environmentally friendly compared to printing posters or leaflets.	• The goods can't be seen or handled before buying. • Customers might not want to disclose personal details on a website. • Technical problems might occur when purchasing something and the customer left wondering if their order has been placed. • No personal contact with the organisation. • Can be expensive to subscribe to an internet service provider. • Can be expensive to make and maintain a website. • Employees need training to maintain and update the website.

> **⚠ Watch point**
>
> It is important to be able to give advantages and disadvantages for both the customer and the business when using the internet.

The internet now allows people to interact using **Web 2.0**. This technology allows people to interact with each other through, eg social networking sites such as Facebook and Twitter, blogs and wikis. It is popular with businesses to advertise their products to a large audience and to communicate with customers; they can interact with each other and questions can be asked. The business can post updates to their social networking site at any time of the day and can potentially reach a large number of people very quickly. Sites such as YouTube allow businesses to upload clips demonstrating how a product works and/or provide information about a product, and can be viewed by customers before they decide to buy a product.

Apps

Apps are being more widely used to advertise and promote products. Users simply download the application onto their smartphone or tablet computer and access it at a touch of a button.

Once accessed, apps work in a very similar way to a website; people can look around at different products, read information and buy what they want. The advantages and disadvantages of smartphone applications are very similar to internet websites but also include:

Advantages	Disadvantages
• Don't have to be sitting at a computer or laptop to use; can use it on the move. • Can often use free Wifi to access the internet (eg in a cafe or even on the bus).	• People need to buy a smartphone or tablet computer, which can be expensive. • Training is needed so that the app can be designed and used easily by customers. • The internet connection depends on the location where the smartphone or tablet computer is being used.

Text messaging

Text (SMS) messaging is widely used by businesses to communicate and promote products to customers. Specific customers can be targeted quickly with information.

Advantages	Disadvantages
• Customer receives the message instantly and directly. • Lots of customers can be targeted. • Cheaper than some other methods of advertising.	• Can only include a small amount of text compared to a website. • Customers might receive lots of text messages and begin to feel frustrated or annoyed. • Need to have the mobile phone number of the customer.

E-mail advertising

Many businesses use e-mail to send mailshots to customers. Customers can sign up to a mailing list and be e-mailed with details of special offers, new products and other promotions.

Advantages	Disadvantages
• Customers can sign up to a mailing list and therefore only those interested receive the information. • E-mail can be sent at any time. • The same e-mail can be sent to more than one person at the same time. • Documents and files can be sent as attachments on an e-mail. • E-mail can be sent worldwide instantly at little cost. • Environmentally friendly compared to printing posters or leaflets.	• Some e-mail providers might filter the e-mail into the spam folder and the user might never receive it. • Receiving lots of e-mails from different businesses might become frustrating or irritating for the customer. • Employees might need training. • Viruses can be spread through e-mail.

● Make the link

Technology is changing quickly and businesses can use it to advertise and promote their business. They must respond to changes in the external environment.

Other advertising methods

Other more traditional methods of advertising are still widely used. These include advertising on TV, in newspapers/magazines and on billboards using posters.

Advertising on TV	TV advertising has the potential to reach a large audience because many people watch TV. TV adverts are often shown on certain channels and at certain times of the day, depending on the market segment being targeted.

Advantages	Disadvantages
• Large audiences can be reached. • Adverts can be targeted towards specific segments. • The product can be shown from different angles. • Demonstrations can be given.	• The cost of advertising nationally on TV can be high. • People might not watch adverts – modern technology means people can skip the adverts. • Adverts are usually quite short and people might not have time to take in all the information given.

Advertising in newspapers and magazines	Different types of newspapers are available; some are only available to buy locally and some are only available on a Sunday. Several newspapers and magazines are designed for specific market segments, eg *The Financial Times* for people interested in business.

Advantages	Disadvantages
• The specific location of the customer can be targeted – nationally or locally. • Adverts can be kept by readers for reference later. • Lots of information can be communicated if the advert is large. • A free sample of the product can be given (common in some magazines).	• Not all newspapers are available in colour. • No sound, video or demonstrations of the product can be given. • Some specialist newspapers and magazines can be expensive to buy and also to place an advert in.

Radio and the media	The radio and different media programmes (eg the news or TV programmes) report on the positive and negative activities of a business. This, provided the report is positive, can provide a business with advertising and generate interest amongst customers. Businesses can also pay to have an advert on the radio.

Advantages	Disadvantages
• Free advertising if the report is positive. • National media reports can reach large audiences. • Local radio stations can reach people locally.	• Not all media reports are positive – they also tell people about the negative impact of business. • The whole situation might not be reported by the media; facts might be missed out or be misleading.

Billboards	Billboards are large signs, usually beside a road, that contain a large poster. They usually don't have much text on them and lots of pictures – this is because people don't have time to read them when they are driving!
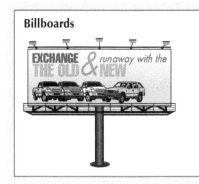	

? Questions

1. Is promotion just about advertising?
2. Name three methods of advertising.
3. Suggest two advantages of internet advertising.
4. Suggest two disadvantages of internet advertising.
5. Explain how a mobile application works.
6. Suggest two advantages of e-mail advertising.
7. Suggest two disadvantages of e-mail advertising.
8. Suggest two advantages of TV advertising.
9. Suggest two disadvantages of TV advertising.
10. What is a billboard?

Promotion methods

Promotion is not just about advertising, it is also about encouraging people to buy a product. Businesses can encourage people to buy a product using different promotion methods.

Special offers

Special offers provide customers with a discount when they buy a product. It might be that they get 10% off a product or they buy one and get one free (BOGOF). Many businesses use special offers to encourage people to buy a product and to encourage them to return to the business. Think about supermarkets – they are full of special offers!

Sometimes businesses will give new customers a special offer to encourage them to try a product for the first time, in the hope that they will continue to buy.

Sometimes special offers are only available to customers through the business website or social networking page. It is becoming more common for special offers to be given out by a business through a smartphone app such as Voucher Cloud.

GO! Activity

In groups, create an advert for a product of your choice.
You can choose to create:

- A webpage
- A short advert
- A poster
- A newspaper article
- An e-mail advert

You could create a website that includes a number of features (eg sound and animation) as well as a form to get feedback from customers. If you create a short advert, you could use mobile technology (eg a phone or tablet computer) to record it and edit it using appropriate software. Be creative!

Once you have finished this task, be prepared to present your findings to your class. Your class will judge how useful each advert is and will give you feedback on:

- **The information communicated** (eg the product name, how it works, what it does, the price, how to order, literacy skills – no spelling mistakes if written down or, if presented orally, communication is professional).

- **The quality of the advert** (does it look professional? Is it informative? Has it been put together well?).

- **The level of teamwork displayed** (you should make sure each member of the group participates and has a role to play when presenting your advert).

You should write down in your learning journal how you think this task went: What went well? What didn't? How would you rate your contribution? What leadership and employability skills did you use?

Skills

- Communication
- ICT
- Enterprise
- Thinking
- Decision making

Free samples

A free sample is a 'taster' of a product. The sample allows people to try a product without having to pay for it.

For example, some perfume shops give out free samples of perfumes for people to try. Without these free samples, customers wouldn't know if they liked the smell of the perfume or not. However, it does cost the business to provide free samples and people might not decide to buy.

Celebrity endorsement

This is when a celebrity is used to promote a business. For example, Jamie Oliver has been used to promote Sainsbury's.

Advantages	Disadvantages
• Customers are attracted to a product because it is associated with a celebrity • Higher prices can be charged as the product is seen as exclusive to a celebrity • Money can be saved on marketing if the celebrity is well known	• Not everyone will like a particular celebrity • The company's reputation could be damaged if the celebrity gets a bad name • Getting a celebrity to endorse a product can be expensive

🔘 Activity

Your teacher will show you how to use a discussion forum for this task.

This task can be done at home. Watch at least two TV adverts – one providing a good and one providing a service. Make notes on the following:

• What the product is.

• What information is being communicated.

• Does the advert stand out? Why?

• How well do you think the advert works? Why?

• Does it use a celebrity to promote the product? Who?

• Does it give details of any special offers? What are they?

Share your findings on a discussion forum with the rest of your class. You could also record your findings in your learning journal.

• Thinking
• Decision making
• ICT

Ethical marketing

Businesses should show that they have an ethical approach to marketing. They can do this by:

• Cutting down on the volume of paper used (eg by printing fewer paper copies of leaflets or posters)

• Not being misleading in the way it presents information in its adverts (eg by not saying 100% of customers like a product if only 5 people have been asked!)

• Complying with discrimination laws and good business practice in its adverts (eg by not using child labour in its adverts or exploiting a vulnerable group of people)

• Ensuring its marketing activities do not offend beliefs that different people may have (eg showing respect to different religions and groups of people based on their age or sexuality)

○ Case study

Reactive Training, Glasgow

Reactive Training, a fitness and sports consultancy business, was started in 2012 by Robert Clarkson. It aims to provide a variety of fitness activities, personal training and sports-related information to its customers in the Glasgow area. Robert's customers come in all shapes and sizes, fitness levels and ages.

Robert started the business because he wanted to make a business idea a reality, to be able to make his own decisions and to have the opportunity to earn extra income. He believes hard work, dedication and being able to communicate with his customers is important when starting a business. Having a good knowledge of the practical skills needed in sport and fitness is also important!

Robert recognised when he started the business that marketing is very important and he felt that this was something he needed to learn about. Through time, he realised that making sure his business is well-known is very important and he has used a number of different promotion strategies.

- Using social networking such as Facebook and Twitter to advertise the business.

- Offering a free personal training session to each customer as a 'taster'.

- Putting up posters in local sports centres.

- Creating a company website.

- Distributing leaflets.

Robert uses e-mail and mobile technology to communicate with his customers, and he believes that social networking has been very useful in gaining new customers.

? Questions

1. Identify the type of business owned by Robert Clarkson.
2. Which sector of industry does Reactive Training belong to?
3. What market segment does Reactive Training target?
4. From the case study, identify two reasons why Robert started Reactive Training.
5. From the case study, identify two qualities needed when starting a business.
6. Suggest an advantage and disadvantage of using social networking.
7. Suggest an advantage and disadvantage of giving a free personal training session to customers.
8. Suggest and justify another method of promotion that Robert could use.

Market research

Businesses have to find out what customers want and what competitors are doing. They have to do this for a number of reasons.

- To make sure they provide the goods and services customers want (otherwise they won't make a profit).

- To make sure that they keep ahead of the competition.

Surveys are carried out as part of market research

Businesses do this by carrying out **market research**. Market research involves looking at information that exists and finding out new information.

There are two types of market research.

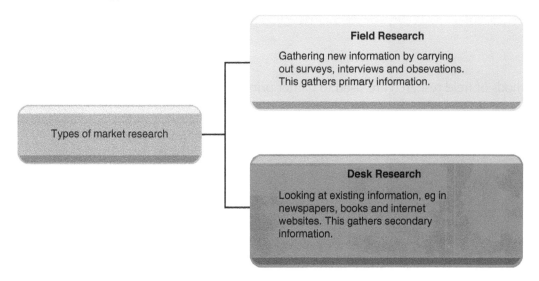

Types of market research

Field Research

Gathering new information by carrying out surveys, interviews and obsevations. This gathers primary information.

Desk Research

Looking at existing information, eg in newspapers, books and internet websites. This gathers secondary information.

There are different advantages and disadvantages of field and desk research.

> ⚠ **Watch point**
>
> Field research gathers primary information and desk research gathers secondary information.

	Field Research	Desk Research
Advantages	• The research has gathered new information and is therefore more up-to-date than existing information. • The information has been gathered for a specific purpose and is therefore more relevant to the business needs.	• Because the research has already been carried out, it is usually easy to obtain by looking in a newspaper, book or on a website. • It is usually cheaper to gather than field research, which saves the organisation money. • Decisions can be made quickly because the information already exists.

	Field Research	Desk Research
Disadvantages	• It can be expensive to carry out field research, which means the money cannot be spent on something else (eg buying a new machine). • It can take a long time to carry out field research, which could stop decisions being made quickly. • People need to be trained in carrying out field research (eg in interview techniques), which can be expensive.	• Because this research was carried out for a different purpose, it is not as reliable as field research and might not be as useful. • The research might have been carried out a long time ago and therefore the information is not relevant to today's business environment. • The information might be biased, which could lead to wrong or incomplete decisions being made.

Make the link

Decision-making is better when high quality sources of information are being used.

Different methods of field research are used to gather primary information.

Personal interview	This involves a face-to-face discussion between two or more people. The interviewer will ask a number of questions.

Advantages	Disadvantages
• The interviewer can encourage the respondent to answer questions. • The interviewer can ask the person being interviewed to clarify a point if they are unsure of something. • Body language and facial reactions can be observed.	• It is time consuming and expensive to carry out. • The interviewer will need training in interview skills. • It is unlikely that the same number of responses would be obtained compared to a survey.

Focus group	A focus group is a discussion between selected people about a specific good or service. People taking part will be asked a number of questions about the good or service with the aim of generating a discussion on these things.

Advantages	Disadvantages
• The feelings and views of people can be observed as can their body language. • Points that are not understood can be clarified.	• It is time consuming and expensive to carry out. • Information can be difficult to analyse. • The sample of people used in the focus group might not represent the views of the whole population.

Postal survey	A postal survey is when a list of questions is sent to people through the post. They will be asked to complete the survey and to send it back to the business.

Advantages	Disadvantages
• It is fairly cheap to send the survey to large numbers of people spread over a wide geographical area. • People can complete the survey at their own pace at a time that suits them.	• People need to open the survey sent to them in the post and send it back; they might not do this. • Can take time to get the information back. • There is no opportunity for the respondent to clarify anything they don't understand. • The survey must be designed carefully so that it is not misinterpreted.

Telephone survey	A telephone survey is when people are contacted by telephone and asked to answer questions.

Advantages	Disadvantages
• Large numbers of people all over the country can be contacted. • It is less expensive to carry out compared to a personal interview. • Information is obtained instantly. • Points can be clarified.	• People might not want to participate in a telephone survey, especially if they have been telephoned at an unsuitable time. • Unsuitable for large surveys as people are often only willing to answer a short survey over the telephone because of the time it would take to respond to a larger one.

Online survey	An online survey is when people answer a number of questions that are displayed on a website. It might involve them clicking on the appropriate answer and/or typing in comments.

Advantages	Disadvantages
• A link to the survey website can be sent to large numbers of people. • Do not need to spend money on printing surveys. • People from all over the world can participate.	• Relies on people having a connection to the internet. • No personal contact.

Hall test 	A hall test involves a product being given to customers to try and then asking for their feedback on it.

Advantages	Disadvantages
• The product is tried by the participant, who can report back on their actual experience. • It is relatively inexpensive to carry out.	• Opinions and views (qualitative information) can be difficult to analyse. • The participant might give the response they think the organisation wants to hear so that they do not come across as being rude.

Observation 	An observation involves watching something and recording what happens. The observer might have to count how many times something happens, or someone does something, or what someone's reaction is to a situation.

Advantages	Disadvantages
• Facts and figures (quantitative information) are gathered, which are easier to analyse than qualitative information. • People being observed might not be aware so should act naturally.	• Those being observed are not usually asked for their opinion or to give an explanation as to why they did or did not do something. • There are privacy and ethical issues to consider when observing people.

Electronic Point of Sale (EPOS) 	EPOS systems gather information when consumers are making a purchase at the checkout.

Advantages	Disadvantages
• Large quantities of information can be gathered. • The information gathered is factual and not just opinions.	• It can be expensive to purchase an EPOS system – especially for a small business. • No opportunity to gain the opinion of the customer.

Social networking website 	Social networking websites such as Facebook and Twitter can be used to gain feedback from people on goods and services. Many businesses use a social networking website to interact with their customers and to find out their reactions and opinions on different issues.

Advantages	Disadvantages
• A two-way interaction occurs between the business and customers. • Large numbers of people can be reached. • Questions can be posed to customers very quickly.	• Customers might not want to join the social networking website of the business. • Information obtained on the website is not usually private and could be viewed by anyone.

GO! Activity

Create a mindmap that shows:

- The different methods of field research and;
- The advantages and disadvantages of each method.

You can create the mindmap on paper or using online mind-mapping software.

- Thinking

GO! Activity

You are going to carry out some market research on the catering facilities provided by your school/college.

You need to decide:

1. Which method of field research to use.
2. What questions to include in your survey (if you choose to do a survey).
3. When you are going to carry out your research.

You should decide these issues in your group and discuss them with your teacher before carrying out your research. Once you have completed your research, write a short report detailing your findings and give it to the canteen manager. You should also be prepared to present your findings to your class. Your class will judge how well you carried out this task and will give you feedback on:

- **Your choice of field research method** (eg was it appropriate? Could you have done anything differently?).
- **Your survey (if appropriate)** (eg was it professional? Were relevant and interesting questions asked?).
- **Your report to the canteen manager** (eg was it useful and did it contain relevant facts? Was it professionally presented? Did it include useful recommendations?).
- **Level of teamwork displayed** (you should make sure each member of the group participates and has a role to play during this task).

You should write down in your learning journal how you think this task went; What went well? What didn't? How would you rate your contribution? What leadership and employability skills did you use?

⚠ Watch point

A questionnaire and a survey are the same thing.

- Research
- Communication
- Decision-making
- Enterprise

❓ Questions

1. What is market research?
2. Why do businesses carry out market research?
3. Identify and describe two types of market research.
4. Describe two advantages of desk research.
5. Describe two advantages of field research.
6. Describe two disadvantages of desk research.
7. Describe two disadvantages of field research.
8. What is qualitative information?
9. What is quantitative information?
10. Describe three methods of field research.

★ Key questions

1. Describe three methods of market research.
2. For each method given in question 1, describe two costs and benefits of each one.
3. Identify and describe the four elements of the marketing mix.
4. Identify and describe the stages of the product life cycle.
5. Suggest ways technology can be used in marketing.

Summary

This chapter provided you with an overview of what marketing is and the different activities involved in the marketing function of a business.

The learning intentions for this chapter were:

- The role of marketing
- Customers and market segments
- The marketing mix
- Market research

By successfully answering the key questions, you will have proved that you have grasped the main topics covered in this chapter.

5 Management of Operations

You should already be able to

- Describe quality measures used by small businesses.
- Describe how operations support a small business.
- Outline how functional areas work together to support a small business.

What you will learn in this chapter

- What is 'operations'?
- Suppliers
- Stock management
- Methods of production
- Quality
- Ethical and environmental

Make the link

The operations department creates wealth by adding value to the product.

What is operations?

The operations function (or department) is responsible for manufacturing products. These products can be tangible or intangible but they are all called products. They do this by processing inputs into outputs during the production process. When they are doing this, value is being added to the product so that profit can be made.

Inputs	Process	Output
The factors of production	The actual making of the product	The finished product ready for sale

Adding value to a product

The operations department carries out a number of different activities:

- They make products. This can involve people or machinery.
- They help satisfy customers by making products that they want.
- They work with suppliers to ensure raw materials are available at the correct time.
- They manage levels of stock to make sure nothing runs out.

Make the link

The operations department uses information from market research to help decide what is made and how it is made in order to satisfy customer needs and wants.

Suppliers

Raw materials are the different items needed to make something. For example, if you were making a cake, your raw materials would be:

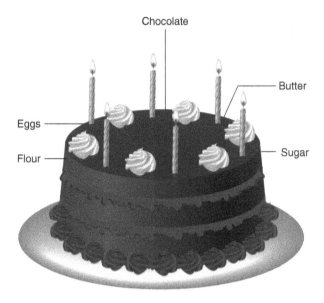

A business has to buy raw materials from a supplier to be able to make something. However there are different factors that will influence which supplier is chosen, just as if you were deciding to buy something from a shop you would take different things into account. These factors are called the **purchasing mix** and include:

Factor	What does this mean?	Why is this important?
Cost of raw materials	The price charged by a supplier to purchase raw materials.	• Costs need to be kept as low as possible to make a profit. • Low costs will improve the cash flow of a business.
Quality of raw materials	How good the raw materials are.	• Without high quality raw materials, the finished product will not be of a high quality. • Low quality raw materials will probably result in higher wastage.
Lead time/ delivery time	How long it will take to receive the raw materials from when an order is placed.	• Some raw materials need to be used quickly (eg fresh food) or they might go off. • Without raw materials being delivered on time, production might have to stop, which is costly.
Quantity of raw materials	How much raw materials are required.	• There need to be enough raw materials available to allow production to continue, however, not too much otherwise this can be expensive for storage. • Correct quantities of raw materials are required to satisfy customer demand.

(continued)

Factor	What does this mean?	Why is this important?
Location of supplier	Where the supplier is located, eg which town or city and how far away it is.	• The further away the supplier is, the longer the raw materials will take to be delivered. • The cost of transporting products has to be considered.
Reliability and reputation of supplier	Reliability – will the supplier deliver when they say they will? Reputation – what people think of the supplier.	• If the supplier does not deliver on time, this might cause production to stop and customers might not get their order on time. • Suppliers with a good reputation are likely to get more business compared to one that has a poor reputation.
Storage space available	How much space the business has in a warehouse to hold the raw materials until they are needed.	• Raw materials might be wasted if they cannot be stored in the correct place. • Storage costs (eg insurance) can be expensive.

Inventory management

Businesses have to manage the stock that they have. Stock includes:

- Raw materials from suppliers.

- Products that are currently being made (work in progress).

- Products that are finished being made.

It is important that stock levels (the number of items stored) are managed. If a business has too much or too little stock, this has consequences.

Consequences of having too little stock

- Production might stop if there are not enough raw materials.

- Customers might not receive their orders on time.

- Unexpected orders cannot be met.

Business have to make sure their raw materials are delivered in time and at a reasonable price

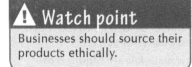

⚠ Watch point

Businesses should source their products ethically.

Stock levels can be managed in a number of ways. Most businesses have a computerised system that records how much stock there is at any one time, eg using EPOS or a spreadsheet package. Many businesses make use of the internet to purchase raw materials. Using technology in stock management enables the business to be 'paper-free', which is good for the environment and also allows stock to be managed more efficiently than by hand; errors are reduced and orders can be placed more quickly with suppliers than with a paper order form.

Consequences of having too much stock

- It costs money to store stock (eg lighting, insurance, security).

- Stock has a higher risk of being stolen.

- Stock has a higher risk of going out of date.

- Money is tied up in stock that could be used for other purposes.

- If social factors change (trends/fashion), the stock might be wasted.

> **⚠ Watch point**
>
> Technology is used in operations in a number of ways. Make sure you are able to describe these.

Inventory control

Businesses might have an inventory (stock) management system in place to manage levels of inventory.

An inventory management system has the following features:

- **Maximum stock level** – the highest amount of stock that can be stored at one time. At this level stock costs will be at the minimum per unit because the organisation is at full capacity.

- **Minimum stock level** – the lowest amount of stock that should be stored at one time. At this level there is a danger that stock levels could fall too low and production would stop.

- **Re-order level** – the quantity at which more stock is ordered.

- **Re-order quantity** – the quantity of stock that has to be ordered to bring levels back to the maximum stock level.

- **Lead time** – the time that passes between ordering stock and it arriving.

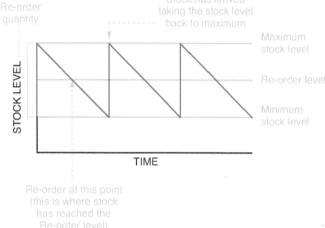

> **⚠ Watch point**
>
> You should be able to draw and label an inventory control diagram.

❓Questions

1. What is the role of the operations department?
2. Name three factors to take into account when deciding on a supplier.
3. What might happen if a supplier delivers late?
4. What does the term 'lead time' mean?

5. What are raw materials?

6. Why do raw materials have to be of a high quality?

7. Describe three consequences of having too much stock.

8. Describe three consequences of having too little stock.

9. What might be the effect on stock of changes in social factors?

10. Where would stock levels be recorded?

Methods of production

⚠ **Watch point**

Production practices should be as ethical as possible (see page 93–95)

Businesses have to decide which method of production to use to make their products. They have to think carefully about how to turn their inputs into outputs.

When deciding which method to use, there are different factors to think about:

- The actual product being made.

- The quantity of the product that needs to be made.

- The way the business will make sure the product is of a high quality.

- The way stock is managed.

- The resources available (eg staff and machinery).

There are three main methods of production: **job**, **batch** and **flow**.

Job production

Make the link

In Hospitality, Health and Food Technology, and Design and Manufacture you will make unique, one-off products using job production.

Job production is when one product is made from start to finish before another one is made. The product is made to the customer's own requirements and this results in a unique or one-off product being made. Products made by job production are usually handmade by someone who is very skilled at what they are doing.

Examples: wedding cakes, handmade chocolates, art, sandwiches being made to order in a sandwich shop.

Advantages	Disadvantages
• The customer gets exactly what they want and this can increase their satisfaction.	• Specialist tools and equipment might be needed, which can be expensive to buy.
• High prices can often be charged because a unique/one-off product is being made.	• Can't always buy raw materials in bulk and might miss out on cost savings from bulk buying.
• Designs can be changed to suit each customer's own requirements.	• Can take a long time to make a unique product and this might mean the employee loses motivation.

Batch production

Batch production is when a group of identical products are made at any one time. All products in the batch move onto the next stage of production at the same time. Machinery and equipment can be cleaned and/or changed between batches to produce a different product.

Examples: cakes, newspapers/magazines, bread.

Advantages	Disadvantages
• Batches can be changed to suit the requirements of the customer, which results in higher customer satisfaction. • Raw materials can be bought in bulk, therefore saving money. • No need for highly skilled workers, so costs are kept down.	• Equipment and employees might not have anything to do between batches, which costs money. • Any mistakes in one item can result in the whole batch being wasted, which costs money and wastes time. • The cost of each item might be high if the batch size is small so the price charged to the customer might be higher.

This picture shows newspapers being made. Today the company will produce one batch before producing a completely new batch tomorrow.

The company might use the same equipment and employees to produce more than one type of newspaper.

Flow production

Flow production is when parts are added to a product as it moves along a production line. The final product will be completed by the time it reaches the end of the production line. Flow production is sometimes called line production. As the product moves along the production line, machinery and workers have very specific tasks to do: one person might screw something in and another might paint a very specific part before moving onto the next task (this is known as **division of labour**).

Examples: cars/vans, computers and other electrical items.

> **⁘ Make the link**
>
> Value is being added to each product as it moves from one stage of production to another.

Advantages	Disadvantages
• Large amounts of identical products are made. • Raw materials can be bought in bulk, saving the business money. • Flow production often uses lots of machinery that can work for longer and without breaks compared to humans.	• The individual customer's requirements cannot be met because each product is identical. • If a fault occurs during production this can cause the whole production line to stop. • Large demand for products is needed because they are made in large quantities.

This picture shows aeroplanes being made on a production line.

As the aeroplane moves along the production line, something else is added to it.

Make the link

Employee motivation can be low when working on production lines because the tasks employees are doing are very repetitive.

Skills

- Communication
- Thinking
- Decision making

Activity

Have a class discussion.

- Make a list of 10 products you commonly use.
- Think about which method of production is used to make these products and why.
- Give at least one reason why it wouldn't be suitable to use a different production method to make them.
- Write down what was discussed for one product in your learning journal.

Skills

- ICT
- Thinking

Activity

For health and safety reasons, it is not often possible to visit a factory to see a product being made. However, you can use YouTube to watch small video clips of products being made. Type different key words into the search bar to find what you are looking for. For example: job production, batch production, flow production, automation. Write a brief outline of what you watched on one video clip in your learning journal.

Skills

- ICT
- Thinking

Activity

Make a mind map showing the different methods of production, including examples and advantages and disadvantages of each method.

Labour and capital intensive

The amount of machinery/equipment and labour used in making a product will determine whether or not it is **labour** or **capital** intensive.

Labour intensive	Products made using mainly human effort.	
	**Advantages**	**Disadvantages**
	• Employees can be creative and use their own initiative. • Labour is usually readily available (though might not always have the correct skills). • No need to purchase expensive equipment. • One-off and unique products can be made easily.	• It is expensive and takes time to recruit, select and train new employees. • Employees require specialist skills, which can take time to learn and may have to undertake training. • The quality of the work can vary depending on who is making it.
Capital intensive	Products made using mainly machines and equipment (in other words, using technology). If a product is made using only machinery, this is known as **automation**. When a mixture of humans and machines are used, this is known as **mechanisation**.	
	**Advantages**	**Disadvantages**
	• Machinery doesn't need breaks – it can work 24/7. • The product being made is of a standardised quality. • Fewer employees are required to be paid. • Employees require fewer skills to work machinery compared to labour intensive production (saves costs).	• Expensive to buy machines and equipment. • Individual customer requirements cannot be met. • Breakdowns can be expensive and cause production to stop.

? Questions

1. Identify and describe three methods of production.
2. Distinguish between capital intensive and labour intensive production.
3. What does the word 'automation' mean?
4. Suggest two advantages and two disadvantages of labour intensive production.
5. Suggest two advantages and two disadvantages of capital intensive production.
6. Name two ways technology can be used in operations.

Quality

Customers want a product that is of the highest possible quality. They want to get the best product they can for the money they pay for the product. This means that the product should work in the way it is designed, should be manufactured using the highest quality raw materials, and should look good. The product should be delivered on time using the correct methods and systems to ensure customer satisfaction (eg after-sales service) should be provided.

The advantages of a business providing a high quality product are:

Make the link

Methods of ensuring customer satisfaction were explored in Chapter 2.

- Customers are more likely to make repeat purchases.

- A good reputation is gained, which will encourage new customers.

- Customers are less likely to buy from a competitor.

- Profit and sales can be maximised.

- The market share of the business can grow.

- Wastage will be minimised, which helps protect the environment.

- Easier to recruit staff to work in a business with a good reputation.

Methods of ensuring quality

Businesses can use different methods to help contribute towards producing a high quality product.

They can:

A bread production line

⚠ Watch point

Make sure you can give advantages and disadvantages of each method as well as describe what it is.

- Use raw materials that are of a high quality.

- Make sure employees have the skills needed to make the product by only recruiting the best employees and by providing training.

- Ensure machinery and other technology is well maintained and regularly checked.

- Use quality control – checking the product at the end of the production process.

- Use quality assurance – checking the product at each stage of the production process

- Use quality management – trying to make sure that every product is made perfectly every time. This requires a commitment by the whole business towards quality.

Method	Advantages	Disadvantages
Using good quality raw materials	• Ensures only the best possible inputs are used.	• Might cost more for quality raw materials. • Requires a reliable and reputable supplier.
Employees	• Fewer errors will be made as employees will know what they are doing. • Accidents less likely to happen.	• Time consuming to train employees – might involve time away from doing the job. • Can be expensive to provide training.
Maintaining equipment	• Any faults are hopefully discovered before they become an even bigger problem.	• Checking equipment regularly might be expensive. • Production might have to stop when machinery is being checked. • Might involve the use of a specialist company.
Quality control	• Less time consuming than quality management.	• Errors are only discovered at the end of the production process – wastage could be high.
Quality assurance	• Errors in production can be spotted quickly	• More expensive to check for errors during production compared to just checking at the end
Quality management	• Product constantly checked to minimise wastage. • More thorough than quality control. • Employees work together on ensuring quality – good for teamwork and motivation.	• Requires commitment from everyone in the business. • Quality policies and procedures need to be implemented and strictly followed.

Ethical and environmental

Businesses have to be **socially responsible**. This means they will be seen in a positive way by not harming the local environment or community.

Businesses can:

- Try to **minimise wastage** by ensuring employees are trained, ensuring machinery is kept in good condition and by not overstocking. However, providing training and maintaining machinery could be expensive.

- **Recycle as much as possible** by encouraging employees to put rubbish in appropriately coloured bins and by re-using materials in the production process as much as possible. Initially buying different coloured recycling bins could be expensive, but they would hopefully encourage people to recycle as much as they can.

- **Try to minimise packaging** by only using the necessary amount of packaging to maintain the product's quality. Not only will this cut down on costs, but it is good for the environment. Using only environmentally-friendly packaging that can be recycled might be more expensive than non-recyclable packaging.

- **Prevent pollution** by watching the materials it uses in production (eg fuel and chemicals) and by disposing of any potentially harmful chemicals or products in the most environmentally friendly way. Businesses that don't dispose of waste carefully can be prosecuted but it is more expensive to prevent pollution than it is to risk prosecution.

Benefits and costs

Businesses that produce products in an ethical way and have an ethical approach to their operations process have their advantages:

- They can gain a good reputation and possible recognition (eg obtain awards)

- Wastage costs can be produced

- Products that are seen as 'ethically produced' can be charged at a higher price

- They can have a competitive advantage over other businesses

But, they also have disadvantages:

- It can be expensive to purchase environmentally friendly materials and fuel

- Suppliers of ethically produced raw materials may charge more

- Training on appropriate waste disposal methods might be expensive

?Questions

1. Suggest three advantages of providing a quality product.
2. Describe three ways a quality product can be produced.
3. Describe an advantage and a disadvantage for each method given in question 2.
4. What does it mean to be 'socially responsible'?
5. Suggest two ways businesses can minimise waste.
6. Apart from minimising waste, suggest two other ways businesses can be environmentally friendly.

Case study

MACKIE'S ICE CREAM, Aberdeen

Mackie's ice cream has been made in Aberdeen since 1986. It is now an employer to over 70 people and has over 500 cows in its herd. It produces a number of different types and flavours of ice cream to specific recipes.

Ice cream is made in batches using a computerised system to carefully monitor the amounts of milk, cream and other ingredients needed to make the ice cream. Products are carefully checked throughout the production process to ensure the highest quality product is made.

The ice cream is packaged in a number of different tubs, depending on the batch and type of ice cream being made. Some tubs are small and suitable for one person whereas some tubs are large and are sold onto other businesses such as restaurants. The tubs are made by Mackie's in Aberdeen to save having to transport them from Sweden, where they were previously made – this is good for the environment as it cuts down on transport pollution. On its website, Mackie's suggests a number of ways people can recycle their old tubs including using them to store paint and to feed birds.

Mackie's is committed to protecting the environment by recycling, making its own tubs, using wind turbines, solar panels and by training staff on the importance of being 'green'.

The Mackie's website contains more information about producing ice cream and also a number of short video clips about its production process.

? Questions

1. Identify the type of production used by Mackie's.
2. Suggest two advantages and two disadvantages of this type of production.
3. Why would job production not be suitable for producing Mackie's ice cream?
4. When is technology used at Mackie's?
5. Give two reasons why it is important Mackie's produces high quality ice cream.
6. Mackie's uses people and machinery in its production process. What name is given to this?
7. From the case study, identify three ways Mackie's help to protect the environment.
8. How does Mackie's production of their own tubs help the environment?
9. Suggest two advantages of being an environmentally friendly business.
10. Suggest three factors a restaurant would consider before deciding to use Mackie's as a supplier. Justify each answer.

Technology in Operations

Technology can be used to support the operations function in a number of ways:

- Internet websites can be used to compare prices of raw materials and to place orders

- Spreadsheets and databases can be used to keep track of inventory levels

- Equipment such as ovens could be pre-programmed to switch on and off at specific times

- Tablet computers could be used to take orders from customers

- Delivery vehicles could contain GPS tracking so that deliveries can be tracked

- CAD – computer aided design – software can be used to design products on screen before they are produced

Case study

BLUEBELL BAKERY, Aberdeen

Bluebell Bakery was set up in May 2011 by Carla Duthie and operates within her home in the Mintlaw area of Aberdeenshire. Bluebell Bakery provides customers with handmade cakes, cupcakes and cake pops. Carla's celebration cakes are her most popular product, and she is slowly moving into the wedding market. She has spent a lot of time trying out new ideas and investing in materials that allow her to follow current trends. Carla's interest in baking began as a hobby before she turned it into a real business.

Questions

1. Bluebell Bakery need to buy raw materials. Describe and justify three factors that need to be taken into account when deciding on a supplier.
2. What type of business is Bluebell Bakery?
3. Identify two products made by Bluebell Bakery.
4. Outline how value is added to Bluebell Bakery's products.
5. Suggest two ways Bluebell Bakery can ensure a quality product is made.
6. Describe an advantage and a disadvantage of each method given in question 5.
7. Suggest two ways Bluebell Bakery can minimise waste.
8. Outline two consequences for Bluebell Bakery if it understocks.
9. Outline two consequences for Bluebell Bakery if it overstocks.
10. Suggest and justify a method of stock control for Bluebell Bakery.

Activity

This is a paired or group activity.

Choose a local business that produces a product and do some research to find out the answers to the following questions:

1. The method of production used and why.
2. The methods used to ensure quality and why.
3. Examples of when technology is used as part of the operations process.
4. Examples of how it is socially responsible (eg by recycling, reducing waste, reducing packaging, etc.).
5. The different jobs that people undertake to make the product.

Once you have finished this task, be prepared to present your findings to your class.

Write down in your learning journal what you have learned.

- Research
- Thinking
- Communication
- Employability

Key questions

1. Describe factors to take into account when choosing a supplier.
2. Describe the consequences of a business overstocking or understocking.
3. Describe factors to take into account when choosing a method of production.
4. Identify and describe ways of providing a high quality product.
5. Suggest ways technology can be used in operations.

Summary

This chapter provided you with an overview of what operations is and the different activities involved in the operations function of a business.

The learning intentions for this chapter were:

- What is operations?
- Suppliers
- Stock management
- Methods of production
- Quality
- Ethical and environmental

By successfully answering the key questions, you will have proved that you have grasped the main topics covered in this chapter.

2 END OF UNIT MATERIAL

Unit assessment

If you are required to do the unit assessment, you need to show your teacher that you have met the learning outcomes and assessment standards for each unit. To do this, your teacher might get you to undertake some tasks at the end of the unit or might get you to gather evidence as you complete the unit. There are a large number of ways you can show that you have met the evidence requirements of the unit and this can vary from unit to unit. The following list gives you an idea of what you might be asked to do.

- Quiz with multiple-choice questions
- Extended-response questions
- An oral presentation
- A mini research project
- A mini project involving creating a blog or wiki
- An information sheet
- A portfolio

To pass the unit assessment, you have to achieve each assessment standard. For this unit, the learning outcomes and assessment standards are:

Outcome 1: Apply knowledge and understanding of how the marketing function contributes to the success of small and medium-sized organisations by:

- Describing methods of market research and outlining their costs and benefits.
- Outlining the stages of the product life cycle.
- Describing elements of the marketing mix.
- Outlining ways ICT can be used to contribute to effective marketing.

Outcome 2: Apply knowledge and understanding of how the operations function contributes to the success of small and medium-sized organisations by:

- Describing the factors to consider when choosing a suitable supplier.
- Describing the consequences of overstocking or understocking for an organisation.
- Describing factors to consider when choosing a suitable production method.

- Outlining methods of ensuring high quality in production practices.

- Outlining how technology can be used to contribute to effective operational activity.

Your teacher will make sure you know what you have to do to pass each unit.

Exam questions: Management of marketing and operations

- Compare labour and capital intensive production. (3 marks)

Make sure you read the question carefully as every word is there for a reason. It is good practice to break the question down into parts before you start to answer it – this will make sure you answer it the best you can.

Compare labour and capital intensive production. (**3 marks**)

The command word – your instruction on how to answer the question.

You must make sure your answer refers to labour and capital intensive production – only writing about one in a compare question would give you no marks.

Sample answer

- Labour intensive production is when lots of humans are used in production **whereas** capital intensive production is when lots of machines are used in production (**1 mark**).

- With capital intensive production, each product is made to the same standard **whereas** with labour intensive production, the quality of the product could vary (**1 mark**).

- Products can be made to individual customer requirements with labour intensive production **but** with capital intensive production they can't because they are all the same (**1 mark**).

Examiner's commentary

It is really important in a 'compare' question that you give both sides (ie labour and capital intensive production) as this is needed to get just one mark! If you only give points for one of them, you won't get any marks at all. In this example, the candidate has bullet pointed their answer and has used the word 'whereas' or 'but' to compare each point they are making carefully – this is excellent. (**3/3**)

- Describe the consequences of overstocking and understocking. (4 marks)

- Give examples of how technology can be used in operations. (3 marks)

- Suggest how other departments might assist the operations department. (4 marks)
- Outline factors to be considered when deciding upon a supplier. (3 marks)
- Describe pricing strategies a business can use. (3 marks)
- Compare field and desk research. (4 marks)
- Describe the following terms:
  - Automation
  - Market growth
  - Test marketing (3 marks)
- Identify stages of the product life cycle. (4 marks)
- Justify the use of technology in promoting a product. (3 marks)
- Describe ways of segmenting a market. (5 marks)

> ⚠ **Watch point**
>
> Look at the marks available for each question as a guide to how long your answer should be.

Check your progress

	HELP NEEDED	GETTING THERE	CONFIDENT
Role of marketing	◯	◯	◯
Market segmentation	◯	◯	◯
The marketing mix	◯	◯	◯
New product development	◯	◯	◯
Product life cycle	◯	◯	◯
Branding	◯	◯	◯
Factors to consider when setting price	◯	◯	◯
Pricing strategies	◯	◯	◯
Business location	◯	◯	◯

	HELP NEEDED	GETTING THERE	CONFIDENT
Distribution methods	◯	◯	◯
Advertising methods	◯	◯	◯
Promotion methods	◯	◯	◯
Desk research	◯	◯	◯
Market research	◯	◯	◯
Technology in marketing	◯	◯	◯
Role of operations	◯	◯	◯
Factors to consider when choosing a supplier	◯	◯	◯
Stock control and inventory management	◯	◯	◯
Methods of production: job, batch, flow	◯	◯	◯
Labour and capital intensive production	◯	◯	◯
Methods of ensuring quality	◯	◯	◯
Ethical production practices	◯	◯	◯
Technology in operations	◯	◯	◯

What actions do you need to take to improve your knowledge?

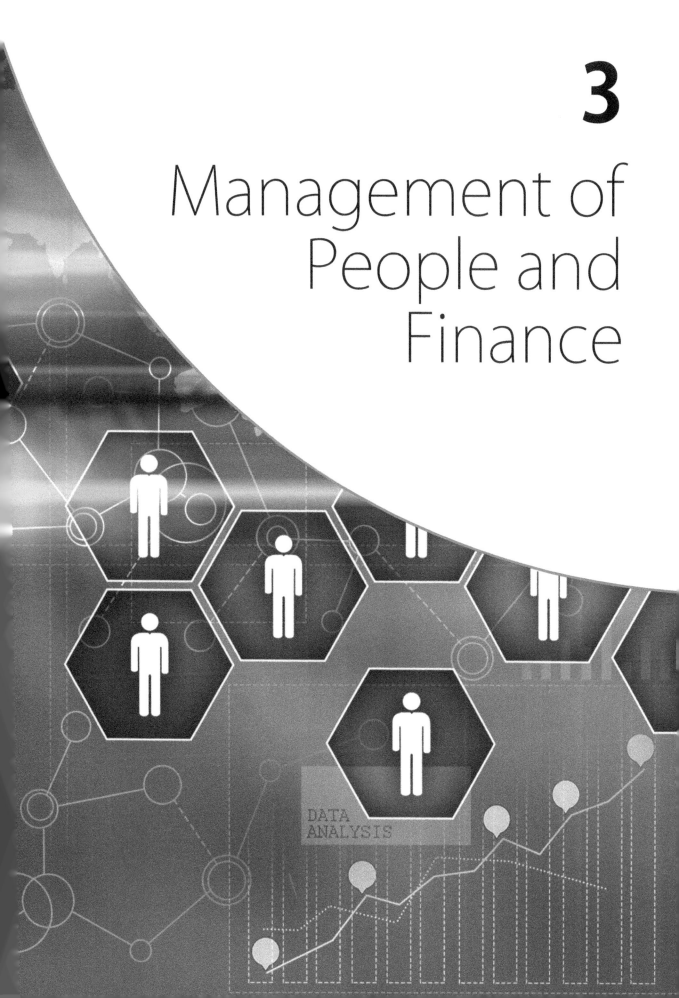

3

Management of People and Finance

6 Management of People

You should already be able to

- Outline the purpose of training employees.
- Describe methods of motivating staff.
- Describe how human resources support a small business.
- Outline how functional areas work together to support a small business.

What you will learn in this chapter

- The role of human resource management
- Recruitment and selection
- Training
- Motivating and retaining
- Legislation

The role of human resource management

The human resource management (HRM) function in a business deals with any issue relating to the management of staff (employees). A business must look after its employees because they play an important role in helping to meet its objectives. The HRM function has a number of activities to carry out.

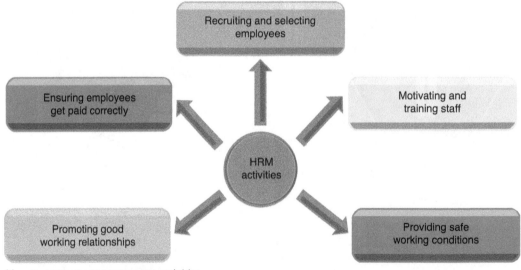

Human resource management activities

Each of these activities are explored in this chapter.

Recruitment and selection

Recruitment and selection are two terms that are often used by people when describing the process of hiring new employees. However, they are different:

Recruitment – encouraging people to apply for a job vacancy.

Selection – choosing the best person for a job.

Recruitment

Recruitment involves encouraging people to apply for a job vacancy. It is important that the best possible people are attracted to work for a business because they play an important role in the business' activities.

- They contribute towards achieving objectives.
- They produce quality goods and provide services.
- They interact with customers and have to provide a quality service.
- They interact and communicate with other stakeholders.

The recruitment process has a number of stages.
Recruitment can take place internally and externally. If internal recruitment is used, **only** staff already employed in the business are able to apply for a vacancy. However, if external recruitment is used, both existing staff and people outside of the business can apply.

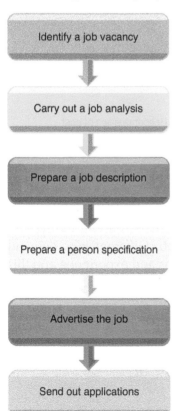

The recruitment process

Identifying a job vacancy

This is the first stage in the recruitment process. This means to check that a job vacancy actually exists; perhaps someone has left the business or the business has expanded and new employees are required. Sometimes job vacancies occur because of periods of high demand or because someone is off work ill.

Carry out a job analysis

The job vacancy is looked at in detail and the tasks, duties and responsibilities that the successful candidate would carry out are considered. This information is then used to construct the job description and person specification.

Prepare a job description

A job description contains information about what the job involves: tasks, duties, responsibilities, pay, working hours, holiday entitlement and any other benefits.

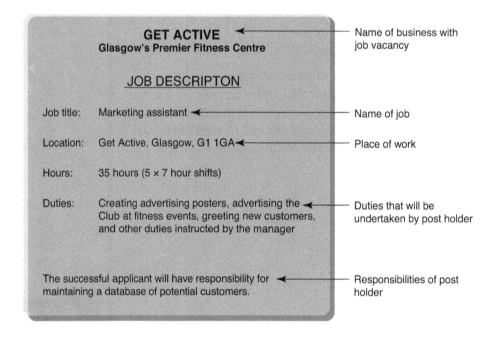

Prepare a person specification

A person specification provides information about the type of person that is required to do the job. Different jobs demand different skills, qualities, qualifications and experience and this document provides details of what is required in a specific job.

The person specification can help in the selection process because it provides a list of what is essential (must have) and what is desirable (ideally would have) for an applicant to have. This can be used to assess how suitable someone is for a job; it can be used as a checklist.

GET ACTIVE
Glasgow's Premier Fitness Centre

PERSON SPECIFICATION
Marketing assistant

	Essential	Desirable
Skills	• Communication • Information technology • Numeracy	• Problem solving
Qualities	• Friendly • Positive attitude • Good timekeeper • Teamworker	• Able to use own initiative • Able to work without supervision
Qualifications	Passes in National 5: • English • Maths • Business Management	• Pass in National 5 Physical Education • First Aid Certificate
Experience	• Working with people in demanding situations	• Work experience in a sports environment

Advertise the job

Before people can apply for a job, they have to know it exists. This is when advertising the job is important – making people aware that a job vacancy exists. A job vacancy can be advertised **internally** or **externally**.

A job could be advertised internally by e-mail, on the business intranet, or by a poster on a notice board.

A job could be advertised externally in a newspaper (locally or nationally), on the business website, via a social networking site, via a recruitment agency or at a Job Centre.

Send out applications

The final stage of the recruitment process is to send out applications. Businesses can ask people to apply for a job in a number of ways:

- By completing an application form (on paper or online).

- By sending a Curriculum Vitae (CV).

An **application form** requires applicants to answer a number of questions that the business has decided. These include questions about the applicant's qualifications, experience, skills and about why they want the job. Questions are sometimes very specific to the job being applied for and sometimes applicants have to describe situations that they have been involved in, eg when working in a team or dealing with a difficult situation.

A **Curriculum Vitae (CV)** is a word-processed document that applicants create themselves. It contains information that the

GO! Activity

Have a look through some newspapers and find two examples of a job advert. Make a note of the information that each advert contains. Which one do you think is better? Why? Stick your job adverts in your learning journal.

- Thinking
- Research

applicant has chosen to include, but would normally contain details of their education, work experience and other achievements. The CV would be submitted by e-mail or sent in the post to the business where the vacancy exists. Sometimes a business will ask applicants to submit a CV in addition to completing an application form.

GO! Activity

The My World of Work website, provided by Skills Development Scotland, gives a variety of career-related information.

Access the My World of Work website and make a note of the information available and resources provided. You could create a personal account so that you can use all of the available facilities.
Make a note in your learning journal of your username (not password!) and a short list of what resources the website has to offer.

? Questions

1. Name three activities carried out by the HRM department.
2. What is the difference between recruitment and selection?
3. Identify the stages of the recruitment process.
4. What happens at each stage of the recruitment process?
5. What is the difference between an application form and a CV?
6. What is internal recruitment?
7. What is external recruitment?
8. Name and describe 2 documents used in recruitment.

Selection

Once applications have been received, the best person for the job has to be selected. First of all, the business would normally look very carefully at each application received (and often references as well) before deciding whether to invite them to the next stage of the selection process or to reject them. This is known as **short-listing** – a list of people who are thought to be suitable for the job based on their application form and references. If invited to the next stage, this would normally involve attending an interview and maybe having to undertake a test.

References

References are a report from a previous employer, school/college about a person. References normally include details about a person's experience, ability to carry out a job, comments on skills/qualities and their attendance record.

Interviews

An interview is a meeting between an applicant and people from the business. The applicant has to answer a number of questions about why they want the job.

Activity

In groups, create a list of questions that you think could be asked at an interview. Using your list, discuss how you might answer each one. Be prepared to discuss your questions with your teacher and class.

- Employability
- Communication
- Thinking

Advantages	Disadvantages
• Personality and appearance of the applicant is seen.	• Time consuming to carry out.
• The content of the applicant's CV or application form can be checked.	• Some people don't perform well at interviews, but might be more than suitable for the job.
• The applicant can ask questions.	• Interviewer bias can exist.

Test

A test can assess a number of things, eg medical, personality or specific skills. Each test will assess a different aspect of the applicant and can confirm the information given on the application form.

Gemma applied for a job as an Administrative Assistant. Her application form says she can type at 40 words per minute. The business asked Gemma to undertake a test to confirm that she can do this.

Advantages	Disadvantages
• The content of the applicant's CV or application form can be confirmed. • Can provide information about the personality of the applicant.	• Time consuming to carry out. • Some people might not be good at tests (they are like exams) because they are stressful.

❓ Questions

1 What is a reference?

2 What is an interview?

3 Give two examples of questions that could be asked at an interview.

4 Give an advantage and a disadvantage of an interview.

5 What is a test?

6 Give an advantage and a disadvantage of a test.

Training

Training is provided by businesses to help people carry out their jobs. Training gives employees the skills and confidence to carry out different tasks to the best possible standard and to do their jobs better. It is of benefit to the business and the individual employee.

There are three different types of training:

• Induction training

• On-the-job training

• Off-the-job training

Training needs are often identified during an **appraisal**; a meeting between an employee and employer that normally takes place yearly. It provides the employee and employer with the opportunity to discuss what is going well, what training is required and what the business can do to help the employee develop and do their job better.

Induction training

New employees are given induction training when they start a job. It provides an introduction to the business and their job. Employees learn about health and safety procedures, the tasks they are expected to carry out, fire evacuation policies and what facilities the business has for staff.

Depending on the number of people starting a job at the same time, induction training might be carried out by one person (eg the manager or owner) or might involve people from different parts of the business.

Advantages	Disadvantages
• Employees become familiar with the organisation and job role more quickly. • Allows the employee to feel part of the business from day one. • It shows the employee that the business is interested in the new employee.	• Could be overwhelming for the new employee. • Time consuming for both the new employee and the person carrying out the induction training.

On-the-job training

This is when training takes place within the business that the person works for. A more experienced employee (a 'peer') might show someone how to carry out a task or the manager might give a presentation to a group of staff on a specific topic.

Advantages	Disadvantages
• Less expensive than off-the-job training. • Creates a good working relationship between the employee and employer. • Training is tailored to the businesses' objectives and needs.	• The employee is still expected to carry out their normal duties. • The quality of training might not be as a high as off-the-job training.

⚠ Watch point

Try to remember some advantages and disadvantages of each training method.

GO! Activity

Do some research to find out what courses are on offer at your local college.

• What courses interest you? Why?

• What courses can you undertake on a part-time basis?

• What entry requirements are there?

• What are the benefits of undertaking a college course?

Note down your findings in your learning journal.

Off-the-job training

This is when training takes place outside the business that the person works for. The training might be provided by a local college or a specialist training company. Off-the-job training might last for a few hours or a few years (eg if a person was undertaking a qualification part-time at college).

Advantages	Disadvantages
• Qualifications can be gained.	• No work is done when people are away undertaking training.
• Training provided by experienced trainers.	• Can be expensive.
• Often provides the opportunity to 'network' – talking to people from other organisations.	• Some off-the-job training can take a long time (eg degrees).

Skills

- Employability
- Research
- ICT

Motivating and retaining

Employees are an important resource for every business; without them, the business would not be able to operate, to meet their objectives and to satisfy customer needs. Motivation of employees is important because it encourages them to work harder.

Businesses can motivate staff by using **financial** and **non-financial** incentives.

- **Financial incentives** – using money to motivate people.

- **Non-financial incentives** – using methods other than money to motivate people.

Having a workforce that is motivated (wanting to work hard) has benefits.

- Staff turnover is lower.

- The quality of the product will be higher.

- Better customer service is provided.

- The reputation of the business is improved.

Businesses that have a workforce that is not motivated might take part in **industrial action** and the quality of the work being carried out would suffer.

Make the link

In Economics and Lifeskills Mathematics you will learn about income and deductions.

Financial incentives

People expect to be paid fairly for the work that they carry out. Different payment systems can be used by a business depending on the activities it carries out.

Make the link

A spreadsheet package can be used to record employee pay.

Salary	Paying a fixed amount of money per year in 12 equal instalments (once every month). The employee knows how much money they will receive each month, but there is no incentive to work harder or produce more. *eg £18,000 salary (12 instalments of £1,500)*
Time rate	Paying per hour worked. The more hours worked, the more pay is received. However, when the employee has not worked many hours, they will not receive as much money. *eg rate of pay is £6.50 per hour and working 30 hours per week (£6.50 x 30 = £195)*
Overtime	Working over the minimum number of hours required per week. Overtime is usually paid at a higher rate than normal, eg time and a half or double-time. The advantage is that overtime is optional, so does not have to be done and allows the employee to earn extra money if they want to. The disadvantage is that it might not always be available, it may depend on demand and seasonal fluctuations.
Piece rate	An amount of money for each item produced in addition to a low time rate or salary. The more items produced, the more money will be earned. Encourages people to work hard and produce more. However, the employee might produce too quickly, in order to get more pay, and the quality of the work might become lower.
Bonus	Receiving an additional payment on top of a salary or time rate. A bonus might be paid for very good work or for meeting a target. Encourages people to work hard.
Commission	A percentage of money paid based on the value of sales a person makes. The more sales made, the more commission is paid. Encourages employees to sell more but might place pressure on the employee to make sales; could cause them stress.

Non-financial incentives

We have already explored two non-financial incentives businesses can use to motivate their employees; training and appraisals.

Other non-financial incentives include:

- Offering flexible working practices.
- Giving people extra responsibilities to encourage them and providing promotion opportunities.
- Praising people for a job done well.
- Allowing people to work in teams and/or take part in team-building tasks.
- Providing training opportunities.
- Providing social events.

Working practices

In today's business environment, people often don't want to work the traditional 9am–5pm, Monday to Friday, working week. This is due to the growth of technology and the number of women in the workplace compared to 20 years ago.

Businesses often offer a range of working practices to satisfy the needs of their employees and to develop good employee relations.

Part time working	Allowing people to work less than full-time hours (which is normally around 35 hours per week).
Temporary contracts	Employing people for a short period of time, perhaps to cover busy periods (eg Christmas) or to cover absences (eg maternity leave).
Homeworking	Allowing people to work from home, using technology to communicate with the business. Employees don't get as much social contact when they work from home but they do get considerable flexibility in deciding when to carry out different tasks.
Teleworking	Allowing people to work away from the office, using technology to communicate with the business. This method relies heavily on technology working.
Job share	Two people sharing one full-time job. One might work the first half of the week and the other the second-half. They might not get a chance to update each other on what they have done and it might cause duplication of work.

Flexible working practices have benefits for the employee and employer.

Benefits to the employee

- Personal commitments (eg family) can be juggled more easily.

- Start and finish times can often be chosen.

- Travelling times can be reduced.

- Less stress as people are in control of their own working time and other commitments.

- Improved happiness and productivity when at work.

Benefits to the employer

- Employees are happier at work and more productive.

- Attendance at work will be improved and staff turnover reduced.

- Can attract more potential employees.

- Space and money can be saved on desks and other facilities.

Industrial action

Creating and maintain good relationships with employees is an important task businesses and their managers have to do. Without it, motivation could be lower and the quality of work poorer.

Businesses can create good working relationships by:

- Consulting with employees on matters relating to them.

- Involving employees in decision making.

- Having an appraisal system, where employees and employer sit and discuss the job they are doing, how well they are doing it and where improvements can be made (this usually takes place once a year).

- Having an 'open door' policy.

- Following the terms and conditions of each employee's contract.

Industrial action can be taken by employees when they are unhappy with their employment terms and conditions or working relationship with their employer.

Strike	Employees refuse to enter the workplace. They might have a picket line or demonstration outside the business to raise awareness of the issues they are facing.
Work to rule	Employees only carry out the tasks and duties written in their job description and no other tasks are performed.
Sit in	Employees refuse to work and 'sit in' the workplace.
Go slow	Employees work slower than normal in order to reduce productivity.
Overtime ban	No hours above the minimum required (as per the employee's contract) are worked.
Boycott	Employees refuse to carry out a new task or to use a new piece of machinery.
Demonstration	A gathering of people raising awareness of a particular issue.

The impact of industrial action can be very serious for a business.

- Production can stop or be slower and this might give the business a bad reputation.

- Customers might be lost to competitors.

- The image and reputation of the business might be damaged.

Industrial action can also have an impact on its employees.

- No pay is received for taking part in industrial action.

- It can be an unsettling and worrying time for employees.

- Relations between the employee and the employer could be damaged.

Case study

PROTEST OVER FURTHER EDUCATION CUTS, Glasgow

Hundreds of College lecturers gathered in Glasgow in May 2017 to voice concern over their terms and conditions. Several speeches were made by several people and leaflets were handed out to pedestrians passing by.

? Questions

1. What type of industrial action is this?
2. What is the aim of the industrial action?
3. What was the purpose of the industrial action?

GO! Activity

In groups, do some research to find an example of industrial action that has taken place recently.

- What type of industrial action was taken?
- Why was industrial action taken?
- What impact did the industrial action have?

Record in your learning journal what you have discovered about industrial action.

Skills

- Employability
- Communication
- Research

? Questions

1. Describe each method of training.
2. For each method given in question 1, give an advantage and disadvantage.
3. What is motivation?
4. Outline three payment methods.
5. Give an advantage of a salary.
6. Give a disadvantage of a salary.
7. Give an advantage of commission.
8. Give a disadvantage of commission.
9. What is the difference between full-time and part-time working?
10. Outline three working practices.
11. Give two benefits of flexible working practices to the employee.
12. Give two benefits of flexible working practices to the employer.
13. Suggest three ways of creating good working relationships.
14. Outline three methods of industrial action.
15. Suggest three consequences to a business of industrial action.

Legislation

Pieces of legislation (laws) are determined by the government and set out different rules and procedures that people and organisations have to follow. There are consequences if the law is not followed.

The Equality Act

The Equality Act brings together a number of different aspects of equality under one piece of legislation. The act aims to prevent against discrimination in terms of different protected characteristics. The protected characteristics are:

- age

- disability

- gender reassignment

- marriage and civil partnership

- pregnancy and maternity

- race

- religion or belief

- sex

- sexual orientation

This applies not just to employees of a business, but also to the people who purchase goods and services from them.

The National Minimum Wage Act

The National Minimum Wage Act (the **National Living Wage**) sets out the lowest amount of pay a person can receive per hour. The current minimum wage (as of April 2020) is:

Age	Rate
25 and over	£8.72
21 to 24	£8.20
18 to 20	£6.45
Under 18	£4.55
Apprentice	£4.15

In Scotland, there is also a **Real Living Wage**. This is an hourly rate that has been calculated to reflect the cost of living today. This Real Living Wage is not compulsory for employers. The current Real Living Wage (at April 2020) is £9.30 per hour. Businesses that pay the Real Living Wage can obtain accreditation to show they are paying more than the National Minimum Wage Act requires.

The Health and Safety at Work Act

The Health and Safety at Work Act sets out the responsibilities employees and employers have concerning health and safety in the workplace. Both have a responsibility to ensure everyone is kept safe and not just themselves.

Employers must:

- Provide relevant health and safety training to employees.
- Provide any necessary equipment and clothing to employees.
- Provide toilets and clean drinking water.

Employees must:

- Comply with the training given by the employer.
- Take care of themselves and other people they work with.
- Report any hazards or accidents that occur.

Techology in HRM

The human resource department will keep a number of records, eg employee personal details and pay details.

A **database** package could be used to record employee personal details. This database would have different fields for each specific piece of information. A database allows you to search for information quickly and to prepare different reports.

A **spreadsheet** package could be used to record employee pay details. See pages 134–135 for more information on spreadsheets.

When keeping records, the human resource department must abide by the **Data Protection Act.** This Act is concerned with the way a business collects, stores, processes and distributes information. It is based on eight principles.

Make the link

Health and safety is important in all parts of life, not just in the workplace.

GO! Activity

Do some research on one piece of legislation and summarise the main principles of it. Present your findings to your teacher in a format of your choice.

Skills

- Employability
- Research

GO! Activity

In groups, carry out a risk assessment of your classroom. Note down in your learning journal any potential hazards that you see and report these to your teacher.

Skills

- Employability
- Thinking
- Communication

Data must:

1. Be obtained fairly and lawfully.
2. Be used for the registered purpose only.
3. Not be used or given to any other person without permission.
4. Be relevant, adequate and not excessive for the required purpose.
5. Be kept accurate and up-to-date.
6. Not be kept for longer than necessary.
7. Be available to the person who it relates to.
8. Be kept secure.

Technology can also be used by the HRM department in other ways. For example, job applications could be submitted online by applicants; interviews and meetings could be held via video-conferencing or Skype and e-mail can be used to confirm appointments that are then scheduled using an e-diary. They may also have an intranet system so that current employees can access relevant HRM information eg HRM policies and forms.

 Activity

Individually, or in pairs, look at the image below and see how many hazards you can find. There are 10 in total. For each hazard, suggest why it is a hazard and what could be done to prevent it.

- Employability
- Decision making

★ Key questions

1. Outline the stages of the recruitment process.
2. Outline the stages of the selection process.
3. Describe three types of training.
4. For each method of training given in question 3, give an advantage and disadvantage of each.
5. Describe ways a business can motivate its employees.
6. Outline two pieces of employment legislation.

Summary

This chapter provided you with an overview of what human resource managements is and the different activities involved in managing people in a business.

The learning intentions for this chapter were:

- The role of human resource management
- Recruitment and selection
- Training
- Motivating and retaining
- Legislation

By successfully answering the key questions, you will have proved that you have grasped the main topics covered in this chapter.

7 Management of Finance

The role of finance

Every business has to manage its money (its finance). Money is important for a business to be able to achieve its objectives, to pay its bills and to keep its owners or shareholders satisfied. Some businesses will have a finance department, whose role it is to manage finance, whereas in a smaller business (eg a sole trader), the owner will be responsible for managing finance.

The role of finance is to:

- Record and maintain financial records, eg cash budgets and income statements.

- Pay bills, eg electricity, insurance and advertising.

- Pay wages and salaries to employees.

Sources of finance

Businesses need money to be able to pay bills, employees and to buy new machinery and equipment. This money might come from sales or it might come from another source.

Sole traders, partnerships and Private Limited Companies have the same sources of finance, except that their ownership capital is different.

- Sole traders are financed by the owner's savings.

- Partnerships are financed by partners (any number between 2 and 20).

- Private Limited Companies are financed by selling shares to family and friends.

A partnership could increase the number of partners to raise additional finance. This means that one or more people would invest in the business and become a new partner, bringing new skills and ideas with them. However, this increases the risk of disagreements occurring and the profits would need to be shared amongst more people.

A Private Limited Company could issue more shares to raise additional finance. This means that there would be more shareholders in the business that can bring large amounts of finance that does not need to be paid back. However, it can be expensive to issue more shares.

Make the link

Pages 19–22 provide more information about each type of business.

Other sources of finance available to each of these businesses are:

Source	Description	Advantages	Disadvantages
Bank loan	A loan of money repaid over time with interest.	• Quick and easy to set up. • Can be repaid over a long period of time.	• Interest could be expensive.
Loan from family or friends	A loan of money from family or friends that does not have interest added.	• No interest to be paid.	• Arguments over the borrowed money might occur.
Government grants	Money from the government that does not have to be paid back.	• Does not need to be paid back.	• Usually has conditions attached. • Can take time to get as requires many forms to be completed.
Bank overdraft	Taking more money out of a bank account than is available.	• Easy and quick to arrange for a short period of time.	• Usually only for a small amount of money. • Daily charges and/or interest applied.
Hire purchase	Buying an item now and paying for it at a later date (often over a period of time).	• Can receive item immediately without paying.	• Interest could make the item expensive. • Item not owned until all payments made.
Mortgage	A special type of loan used to purchase property or land.	• Can be taken out over a long period of time (eg 25 years).	• If interest rates change, repayments might increase.

? Questions

1. Describe three sources of finance.
2. Suggest an advantage and a disadvantage for each source identified in question 1.

Break-even

Most businesses have the aim of making a profit. To be able to make a profit, the money made from selling products has to be more than the money paid out in expenses (costs).

Profit = sales – expenses

Businesses work out the break-even point to find out how many units of a product they have to sell before they start to make a profit. The break-even point is when:

Total costs = Total revenue

Types of costs

Costs is another name for expenses; money going out of the business. We need to know about three types of costs: fixed, variable and total costs.

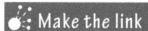

Make the link

Depending on the payment system used, labour costs could be fixed or variable.

⚠ Watch point

Make sure you can describe each cost and give examples.

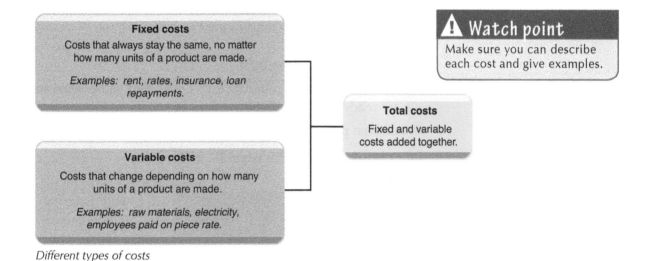

Fixed costs

Costs that always stay the same, no matter how many units of a product are made.

Examples: rent, rates, insurance, loan repayments.

Total costs

Fixed and variable costs added together.

Variable costs

Costs that change depending on how many units of a product are made.

Examples: raw materials, electricity, employees paid on piece rate.

Different types of costs

ROB'S JOINERY

Rob has a joinery business making and selling wooden tables. He has fixed and variable costs to pay.

Fixed costs – £200 per week (eg rent on a shed, bank loan repayment and insurance on his van).

Variable costs – £5 per table (eg cost of wood, glue and paint).

Rob's costs would be:

Number of units (tables made)	Fixed costs (FC)	Variable costs (VC)	Total costs (TC)
0	£200	£0	£200
1	£200	£5	£205
2	£200	£10	£210
3	£200	£15	£215
4	£200	£20	£220
5	£200	£25	£225

Revenue

Revenue is the name given to money that a business receives through selling a product. The more products sold, the higher the total revenue (TR) will be.

Total revenue = selling price × units sold

Rob sells each table he makes for £25. If he sells 10 tables in one week, he will have made a total revenue of £250.

Calculating break-even

We now know how to calculate total costs and total revenue so we are ready to work out the break-even point:

Break-even point (BEP) = Total costs (TC) = Total revenue (TR)

Rob's break-even point is when TC = TR.

Number of units sold	Total costs (TC)	Total revenue (TR)
0	£200	£0
1	£205	£25
2	£210	£50
3	£215	£75
4	£220	£100
5	£225	£125
6	£230	£150
7	£235	£175
8	£240	£200
9	£245	£225
10	£250	£250
11	£255	£275
12	£260	£300
13	£265	£325

Rob will have to sell 10 tables every week to break even (TC=TR).

He does not start making a profit until he has sold 11 tables. When he sells 11 tables, he makes £20 profit (£275 - £255 = £20).

We can use the information in the table opposite to create a break-even chart. A break-even chart shows us how costs and revenue change depending on the number of units sold.

The break-even chart shows us that:

- The break-even quantity is 10 units.

- A total revenue of £250 is needed to break-even.

- When only 0-9 units are sold, a 'loss' is made (total costs are greater than total revenue).

- When 11 or more units are sold, a 'profit' is made (total costs are less than total revenue).

⚡ Make the link

Different marketing strategies can be used to increase total revenue.

Skills

- Thinking
- Decision making

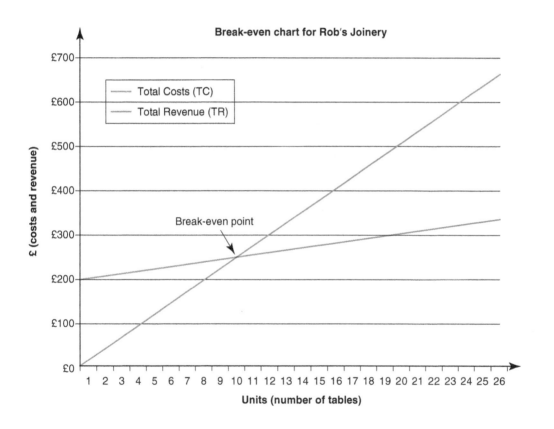

Break-even chart for Rob's Joinery

GO! Activity

Cars R Us manufacture quality sports cars.

Look carefully at the break-even chart below and answer the questions that follow.

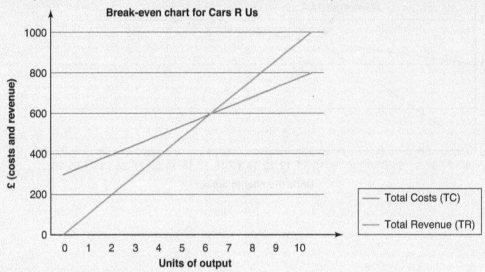

1. What is the break-even quantity?
2. What is the total revenue required to break-even?
3. How much profit is made at 11 units of output?
4. How much profit is made at 3 units of output?
5. What is the selling price per unit?

Activity

Katie owns her own business, making and selling cakes. She has a number of fixed and variable costs to pay before she can make any profit.

Every month, she has £300 fixed costs and each cake costs £3.00 to make. She sells each cake for £10.00

Copy and complete the following table.

Number of cakes	Fixed costs	Variable costs	Total costs	Total revenue	Profit or loss
0					
5					
10					
15					
20					
25					
30					
35					
40					
45					
50					

Using the information in the table, construct a break-even chart. You can do this on paper or using a spreadsheet package.

1. Give an example of a fixed cost Katie would have.
2. Give an example of a variable cost Katie would have.
3. Suggest two ways Katie could increase revenue.
4. Is a profit or a loss made at 10 units?
5. Is a profit or a loss made at 45 units?
6. How many cakes does Katie need to produce to break-even?
7. What is the total revenue at the break-even point?

? Questions

1. What is the break-even point?
2. What are fixed costs?
3. Give an example of a fixed cost.
4. What are variable costs?
5. Give an example of a variable cost.
6. How is profit calculated?

- Numeracy
- Thinking
- Decision making

Cash budgeting

Cash is an important resource for any business because without it bills would not get paid and staff would not get paid. Cash is needed on a day-to-day basis to operate.

Cash flow (the amount of cash in a business) has to be carefully monitored. Businesses that do not have a healthy cash flow can face problems.

Poor cash flow can be caused by:

- Spending too much money on stock that has not sold.

- Giving customers too long to pay their debts.

- Not receiving enough money from sales.

- Not receiving enough time to pay bills from suppliers.

- Owners taking too much money out of the business (drawings).

Businesses can improve cash flow by:

- Looking for cheaper supplies of raw materials as this would reduce the variable costs of making a product.

- Selling equipment or machinery no longer needed as this will bring in cash that can be used to fund other activities.

- Increasing marketing activities as this will raise awareness of the products the business has to sell and increase sales.

- Offering discounts to customers who pay on time as this will encourage them to pay more quickly.

- Taking out a bank loan and paying it back over a period of time.

Make the link

Sources of finance can be used to solve short-term cash flow problems.

Make the link

Budgeting is important in life as well as in business.

Cash budgets

A cash budget is a document that can be prepared to help manage cash flow. It contains a list of cash the business expects to receive (receipts) and the cash expected to be paid out of the business over a period of time (payments). It allows the business to plan for the future and to help make financial decisions.

The benefits of preparing a cash budget are:

- To show if the business will have a surplus (more cash expected to come in than will go out) or deficit (more cash expected to go out than will come in) of cash.
- It can show if additional finance is required, eg overdraft or loan.
- It can help control expenses by highlighting periods when expenses could be high.
- It can help in making decisions.

> **⚠ Watch point**
>
> Cash budgets are a forecast (a plan) of what cash is expected to come in and go out.

Rob has prepared a cash budget for October–December. He wants to make sure that he will have enough cash coming in to cover his expenses.

Cash budget for Rob's Joinery for October–December

	£ October	£ November	£ December
Opening balance	100	190	185
Receipts			
Sales	200	120	110
Total receipts	200	120	110
Cash available	300	310	295
Payments			
Purchases	50	60	70
Advertising	30	30	20
Wages	20	25	30
Rent	10	10	10
Total payments	110	125	130
Closing balance	190	185	165

Annotations:
- The cash available at the start of the period → Opening balance
- Money expected to come in → Total receipts
- Opening balance + receipts → Cash available
- Money expected to go out → Total payments
- Cash available less total payments → Closing balance

We can tell a lot from Rob's cash budget:

- Sales are decreasing.
- Purchases are increasing.
- Wages are increasing.
- Total payments are increasing.
- The closing cash balance each month is decreasing.

⚠ Watch point

You need to be able to interpret a cash budget.

Rob would need to investigate to see why sales are expected to go down – perhaps he needs to do some marketing. Some expenses are also going up (eg purchases) – perhaps he needs to try and find a cheaper supplier.

🔵 Activity

Using the following information, prepare Katie's cash budget for January–March.

- Sales for January £300, February £200 and March £180.
- Purchases for January £150, February £200 and March £210.
- Insurance is £40 for each month.
- Wages are £80 for January and February, but wages in March are expected to be 10% higher than February.
- Loan repayment is £50 each month.

Cash budget for Katie for January-March

	£ January	£ February	£ March
Opening balance			
Receipts			
Sales			
Total receipts			
Cash available			
Payments			
Purchases			
Insurance			
Wages			
Loan repayment			
Total payments			
Closing balance			

Using your completed cash budget, answer the following questions:

1. Comment on Katie's cash budget for January–February.
2. Suggest appropriate action Katie could take to solve any problems identified in question 1.

🌳 Skills

- Numeracy
- Thinking
- Decision making

? Questions

1. What is a cash budget?
2. Suggest three reasons why businesses prepare a cash budget.
3. What does the term 'receipts' mean?
4. What does the term 'surplus' mean?
5. Suggest three causes of poor cash flow.
6. For each suggestion in question 5, suggest a way of improving cash flow.

Income Statements

An income statement is prepared to show gross profit and profit for the year. It can help the business to make decisions, for legal reasons and to help calculate the amount of tax to be paid.

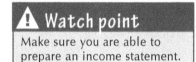

⚠ Watch point

Make sure you are able to prepare an income statement.

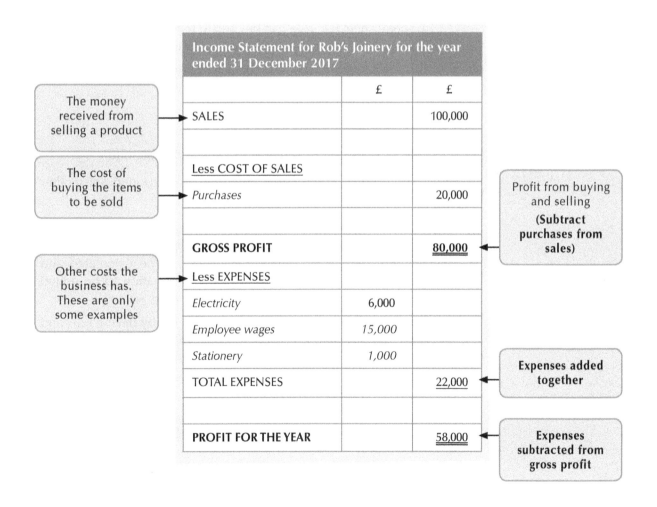

The money received from selling a product

The cost of buying the items to be sold

Other costs the business has. These are only some examples

Income Statement for Rob's Joinery for the year ended 31 December 2017		
	£	£
SALES		100,000
Less COST OF SALES		
Purchases		20,000
GROSS PROFIT		80,000
Less EXPENSES		
Electricity	6,000	
Employee wages	15,000	
Stationery	1,000	
TOTAL EXPENSES		22,000
PROFIT FOR THE YEAR		58,000

Profit from buying and selling
(Subtract purchases from sales)

Expenses added together

Expenses subtracted from gross profit

Skills

- Communication
- Thinking

 Activity

As a class, create a graffiti wall displaying as many different expenses as you can.

Activity

Using the data provided, prepare Katie's income statement.

Sales	£300,000	Heating	£10,000
Wages	£30,000	Advertising	£5,000
Insurance	£6,000	Purchases	£40,000

1. Has Katie made a profit or a loss?
2. Suggest two ways Katie could improve her profit.
3. Suggest some other expenses that Katie might have.

Skills

- Numeracy
- Thinking
- Decision making

Make the link

In Administration & IT you will learn how to create a spreadsheet for different purposes.

Technology in finance

A spreadsheet package can be used to record and edit numerical information. A spreadsheet (eg Microsoft Excel) could be used to:

- Record cost information and calculate break-even.
- Prepare cash budgets.
- Prepare income statements.
- Create graphs showing income and expenditure.
- Prepare information that can be exported into other packages (eg word processing).

The user can enter formulae into the spreadsheet to perform various calculations. Numbers can be added, subtracted, divided, multiplied, different statistics can be calculated and graphs can be created. It allows for information to be edited quickly and saved to be used at another time.

Businesses can carry out banking online (eg by paying bills and arranging overdrafts). Lots of banks have very detailed websites that provide access to a range of information on loans, different types of bank accounts and other sources of finance.

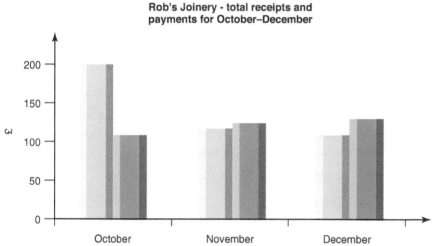

The spreadsheet on the left shows Rob's cash budget.

The figures are arranged in individual cells.

The spreadsheet on the right shows **formulae** that has been entered to calculate different figures in the cash budget.

Rob's Joinery - total receipts and payments for October–December

This graph has been created using the total receipts and payment figures from the spreadsheet.

It compares these figures for each month.

Graphs make comparisons of numerical information easier to see at a glance.

- Total receipts
- Total payments

?Questions

1. What is the difference between gross and net profit?
2. How is gross profit calculated?
3. Give three examples of expenses a business might have.
4. What package might be used to prepare financial information?
5. Suggest three benefits of using this package.

Make the link

Graphs are frequently used in Mathematics and in Science.

Activity

Record in your learning journal the different words you have learned in this chapter. Note some of the benefits of using a spreadsheet package to record financial information.

- Thinking

135

Activity

Using your answers to the cash budget exercise (page 132) and income statement exercise (page 134), create a spreadsheet using these figures.
Enter formulae where you can (ask your teacher for help if you aren't sure).

Skill

• ICT

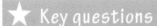

★ Key questions

1. Describe sources of finance that could be employed by a private sector business.

2. Give a definition of each of the following terms:
   • Fixed costs
   • Gross profit
   • Variable costs
   • Surplus
   • Break-even point
   • Deficit
   • Net profit

3. Describe the purpose of preparing a cash budget and an income statement.

4. Give reasons why a spreadsheet could be used to prepare financial information.

Activity

Create a graph, using a spreadsheet, showing Katie's total receipts and payments for January–March (page 134).

Skill

• ICT

Summary

This chapter provided you with an overview of what finance is and the different activities involved in managing the finance function of an organisation.

The learning intentions for this chapter were:

• The role of finance

• Sources of finance

• Break-even

• Cash budgeting

• Income statements

• Technology in finance

By successfully answering the key questions, you will have proved that you have grasped the main topics covered in this chapter.

3 End of Unit Material

Unit assessment

If you are required to do the unit assessment, you need to show your teacher that you have met the learning outcomes and assessment standards for each unit. To do this, your teacher might get you to undertake some tasks at the end of the unit or might get you to gather evidence as you complete the unit. There are a large number of ways you can show that you have met the evidence requirements of the unit and this can vary from unit to unit. The following list gives you an idea of what you might be asked to do.

- Quiz with multiple-choice questions
- Extended-response questions
- An oral presentation
- A mini research project
- A mini project involving creating a blog or wiki
- An information sheet
- A portfolio

For this unit specifically, you will be required to interpret and prepare financial information as indicated in the assessment standards below.

To pass the unit assessment, you have to achieve each assessment standard. For this unit, the learning outcomes and assessment standards are:

Outcome 1: Apply knowledge and understanding of how the management of people contributes to the success of small and medium-sized organisations by:
- Describing stages of the recruitment process.
- Describing methods of training and outlining their costs and benefits.
- Examining methods of motivating staff and outlining their costs and benefits.
- Outlining current employment legislation.

Outcome 2: Apply knowledge and understanding of how the management of finance contributes to the success of small and medium-sized organisations by:
- Describing sources of finance and outlining their costs and benefits.
- Interpreting a break-even chart.

- Interpreting a cash budget to identify cash flow issues and outlining appropriate solutions.
- Preparing a simple income statement from data provided.

Your teacher will make sure you know what you have to do to pass each unit.

Exam questions: Management of people and finance

- Businesses have to comply with the law. Identify and describe two pieces of legislation. (4 marks)

Make sure you read the question carefully as every word is there for a reason. It is good practice to break the question down into parts before you start to answer it – this will make sure you answer it the best you can.

Businesses have to comply with the law.

Identify and describe two pieces of legislation. (4 marks)

This sentence helps to set the scene for the question.

The command words are instructions on answering the question. Note this question has two command words.

Must give two pieces of legislation to be able to get the available marks.

Sample answer

- The Data Protection Act **(1 mark)**. This Act sets out different principles that a business has to follow when storing and distributing information. **(1 mark)**

- The Equality Act **(1 mark)**. This Act brings previous pieces of legislation relating to equality (eg race, sex and age) together. People must be treated equally. **(1 mark)**

Examiner's commentary

The candidate has read the question very carefully. They have identified (named) two pieces of legislation and have then described each piece, one at a time. Had the candidate only named pieces of legislation (without giving more details about what they are about) they would only have gained 2 marks. **(4/4)**

- Describe steps in the recruitment process. (3 marks)
- Describe ways of motivating employees. (3 marks)

- Suggest advantages to the employee and employer of flexible working practices. (4 marks)
- Justify why businesses should train their employees. (3 marks)
- Describe the terms gross and operating profit. (2 marks)
- Suggest reasons why a business might experience cash flow problems. (3 marks)

Check your progress

	HELP NEEDED	GETTING THERE	CONFIDENT
Role of human resource management	◯	◯	◯
Recruitment	◯	◯	◯
Selection	◯	◯	◯
Training	◯	◯	◯
Motivating and retaining	◯	◯	◯
Industrial action	◯	◯	◯
Legislation	◯	◯	◯
Technology in managing people	◯	◯	◯
Role of finance	◯	◯	◯
Sources of finance	◯	◯	◯
Break-even and costs	◯	◯	◯
Cash budgeting	◯	◯	◯

	HELP NEEDED	GETTING THERE	CONFIDENT
Income statements	◯	◯	◯
Technology in finance	◯	◯	◯

What actions do you need to take to improve your knowledge?

Answers

The role of business (page 12)

1. Needs are essential for survival whereas wants are not.

2. Food, clothing, water, shelter.

3. Anything non-essential, eg holidays, mobile phone, DVD, computer game.

4. Those living in developing countries and people who are homeless.

5. A good is tangible (can be picked up) whereas services are intangible (can't be picked up).

6. Goods – a computer, a newspaper, a can of juice, a CD.

   Services – internet access, TV programme, getting a haircut, a train journey, being taught.

7. Durable goods can be used more than once whereas non-durable goods can only be used once.

8. Making something.

9. Using something up.

10. By carrying out market research.

11. To make a profit.

Sorted case study (page 18)

1. Both – service is arranging the event and goods include the chocolate fountain, balloons, etc.

2. Tertiary

3. Combines the factors of production.

4. Risk-takers, hard workers, good communicators, make decisions, are creative, problem-solving, motivated, have confidence.

5. A hobby, interest, through market research, talking to others.

6. No demand for it, losing investment.

7. To provide a good/service, to maximise profit, to satisfy customers.

The role of business (page 19)

1. The resources that are combined together to make something.

2. Land, labour, capital and enterprise.

3. Land – natural resources, labour – the workforce, capital – man-made resources, enterprise – combining the factors of production.

4. The entrepreneur.

5. Communication, decision-making, risk taking, motivating, people skills.

6. Adding value to a product as it moves from one stage of production to another.

7. Primary – taking raw materials from the ground, secondary – using raw materials to make something, tertiary – providing a service.

8. Primary – Forfar Potato Farmer, Arbroath Smokie Farmer.

   Secondary – Clyde Shipbuilders, Stirling Builders.

   Tertiary – Tourist Information Centre, Scottish Exhibition & Conference Centre, Hilton Hotel, O2.

Types of business organisations (page 27)

1. Private, public, third.

2. Sole trader – owned by one person, Partnership – owned by 2–20 people, Private Limited Company – company owned by shareholders who are invited.

3. A sole trader is owned and controlled by one person (the sole trader) whereas a Private Limited Company is owned by shareholders but controlled by a Board of Directors.

4. A disagreement might result in communication being slow or non-existent between the partners for a period of time and therefore decisions may not be made quickly.

5. Limited liability, ability to raise finance through selling shares, experience/skills of shareholders and managers.

6. The Scottish Government.

7. Emptying bins (waste collection), providing leisure facilities and running schools.

8. An organisation with a social or environmental aim.

9. The legal structure is different and charities have more regulation than a social enterprise.

10. Grants and donations.

Objectives (page 30)

1. A document that lets customers know about the level of service to be provided and if they make a complaint how it will be dealt with.

2. Encourages customer loyalty, gives the business a good reputation, helps to maximise sales and profit, can increase market share.

3. To continue trading.

4. Profit = Income – Costs

5. To encourage customers to return to the business.

6. Number of customers a business has.

7. To be seen in a positive way by not harming the local environment or community.

8. The business with the most customers in a market.

LC Personal Training case study (page 30)

1. Sole trader

2. Lee Coutts

3. Service – intangible product being offered by someone who has specialist knowledge and training.

4. Tertiary sector

5. Land – the human body/air/water, Labour – Lee Coutts Capital – equipment used when training, Enterprise – idea developed by Lee Coutts.

6. To fulfil a love of gym training, to see people grow in confidence and achieve their goals.

7. No customers/lack of demand, which means no income coming in and the business failing.

8. Provide more than one service (one-to-one personal training and online advice).

9. Passion for fitness, motivated by others reaching their goals, learning from experiences, dedicated, hard working.

10. To ensure the best possible service provided and customers get the best results.

11. Survival – as money was going out but not coming in.

12. This means that customers are happy with the service they are getting.

13. To make profit, to ensure customers come back, to reduce the risk of business failure.

14. Yes – because it's a private sector business.

Simpsons Garden Centre case study (page 37)

1. To be socially responsible.

2. To ensure staff understand the reasons behind being an environmentally friendly business and so follow their environmental policy.

3. Sensors pick up on movement and lights only go on when necessary – cutting electricity wastage.

4. Less transport pollution, ie less distance to travel.

5. To reduce water wastage.

Influences on business: external factors (page 38)

1. Political, social, technological, competitive, political, economic, environmental, environmental, social.

2. UK Parliament, Scottish Government, local authority.

3. Introducing a new law, changing taxes.

4. When the amount of money being spent on goods and services gets low and the quantity of products being sold decreases.

5. Low – encourages people to borrow money and to spend rather than save.

6. By doing market research.

7. To interact and communicate with other people.

8. Recycle, reduce carbon emissions, increase use of environmentally friendly products, decrease pollution.

9. A business offering the same or similar product.

10. More choice, cheaper goods, more special offers, higher quality service.

Influences on business: internal factors (page 41)

1. A person or group of people with an interest in the success of the organisation.

2. Owners, shareholders, employees, banks, local community, government, suppliers, customers.

3. Employees, suppliers, banks, national government, pressure groups, local community, customers.

4. Local community, shareholders, customer, local council, local community, bank, supplier.

Customer and market segments (page 54)

1. Marketing involves trying to meet the needs and wants of customers. It does this by finding out what they want and providing this at a price that allows a company to make a profit.

2. Where customers (the buyer) and sellers (the supplier) come together.

3. Goods and services to customers.

4. On the internet, in a shop, over the telephone, on a mobile phone, tablet computer.

5. Yes

6. Because it lets customers know that products are available to buy.

7. By entering new markets (eg on the other side of the world).

8. Increasing the number of customers a business has.

9. The proportion of customers a business has from the whole market.

10. The business with the most customers in a market.

11. Its market share will decrease.

12. A group of people with a common characteristic/feature.

13. Gender, age, occupation, religion/cultural belief, income/social class, geographical location, lifestyle.

14. The product (toys) is marketed to people of a certain age – in this case, children.

15. The product (running shoes) is marketed to people who lead a particular life – in this case, participate in running.

Vincent Barbers case study (page 57)

1. Tertiary – providing a service.

2. Men

3. To ensure the product is specific to the needs of the customer group (ie men), so that customers can access it in the most appropriate place, so that a price can be set to reflect the segment, so that advertising and promotions are targeted towards the correct customer group.

4. Hair cut, massage, shaving.

5. Hair wax, shampoo, body wash.

6. To encourage loyalty/repeat purchases, to achieve objectives, to increase sales, to beat competition.

7. In a shop in the city centre of Glasgow.

8. Advertising on a website, special offers for grooming packages, advertising on Facebook.

The marketing mix (page 57)

1. The marketing mix consists of four elements that help a business to achieve its marketing objectives.

2.

   - The way customers are informed that a product exists – PROMOTION.

   - The amount of money being charged for the product – PRICE.

   - Where the customer can buy the product – PLACE.

   - The good or service being sold – PRODUCT.

3. They carry out market research.

4. Product – must be what customers want or customers will not buy it. Price – price must reflect the quality of the product (not too high) or customers will shop somewhere else. Place – product must be accessible. Promotion – customers need to know the product exists so they can buy it.

Product (page 62)

1. Market research carried out, gather product ideas, create prototype, test market product, make necessary changes, decide method of production/price/place/promotion methods.

2. Where customers get to try out the product and provide feedback.

3. No demand, damaged business reputation, external factors, wasted investment.

4. Introduction, growth, maturity and decline.

5. Introduction

6. Maturity

7. Decline

8. A logo, name or symbol that is given to a group or type of product.

9. Recognisable to customers, can encourage loyalty, higher prices can be charged, associated with quality, easier to introduce new products.

10. Reputation of business can be damaged because of one poor product, fakes can be produced, time consuming/lengthy process.

Price (page 64)

1. Life cycle, competitors prices, cost of making profit, profit wanted, ability to supply, product's market segment.

2. Low price, high price, promotional, psychological, cost-plus.

3. The cost of making the product is worked out and a % of profit is then added on.

4. To cover all costs.

5. Price will be reduced so that the product sells.

6. Customers think that the product is cheaper and therefore buy it.

Place (page 68)

1. Where the customer is, availability of premises, parking, infrastructure, government incentives, market segment, employee availability, competition.

2. Infrastructure refers to the availability of water, gas, electricity and transport links.

3. Employees might be needed to work in the business and therefore employees with suitable skills need to be available nearby.

4. To meet its aim of being socially responsible, to ensure it maintains a positive image.

5. Often cheaper than other methods, delivery is often quick, customer receives the product direct to their door.

6. Large amounts of small products can be transported, products can be transported across the world more quickly than by sea.

7. No. Not all products are tangible goods – some might be provided electronically via the internet.

Promotion (page 73)

1. No

2. Advertising on websites, smartphone apps, e-mail, text messaging, TV, magazines, posters/billboards, media/radio.

3. See page 69.

4. See page 69.

5. People need to buy a smartphone or tablet computer and download the application. When downloaded, the user can click on the app to access specific information about a business or product.

6. See page 71.

7. See page 71.

8. See page 72.

9. See page 72.

10. Large signs, usually beside a road, that contain a large poster.

Reactive Training case study (page 76)

1. Sole trader

2. Tertiary

3. Anyone with an interest in fitness and improving fitness.

4. To make a business idea a reality, to be able to make his own decisions and to have the opportunity to earn extra income.

5. Hard work, dedication, being able to communicate, practical skills.

6. See pages 69 and 80 for answers.

7. See page 76 for answers.

8. Any suitable method from pages 76–77.

Market research (page 82)

1. Finding out what customers want and what competitors are doing.

2. To make sure they provide the goods and services customers want, to make sure that they keep ahead of the competition.

3. Desk – looking at information that already exists, field – gathering new information.

4. Easy to obtain, usually cheaper to gather than field research, information already exists so quick decisions can be made.

5. New/up-to-date, for a specific purpose so therefore more relevant.

6. The information was gathered for a different purpose, the information is older, could be biased.

7. Expensive and time consuming to carry out, training to carry out field research could be expensive.

8. Opinions, views and feelings.

9. Facts, figures and numbers.

10. Any three methods from pages 78–80.

What is operations? (page 87)

1. To manufacture (make) products.

2. Any three from pages 85–86.

3. Production might stop and orders wouldn't get fulfilled.

4. The time it takes the supplier to deliver once an order has been placed.

5. The materials that go into making a product.

6. If raw materials are not of a high quality, the final product will not be of a high quality.

7. Any three from page 87.

8. Any three from page 86.

9. Stock might be wasted, if it is no longer wanted.

10. On a computerised system: EPOS or spreadsheet package.

Methods of production (page 91)

1. Job – one off/unique products, batch – group of identical products made at a time, flow – product moves along a production line with parts being added at each stage.

2. Capital intensive – use of machinery/equipment in production, whereas labour intensive – use of humans in production.

3. Products made usually by machines only – very capital intensive.

4. Any from page 91.

5. Any from page 91.

6. EPOS or spreadsheet package for stock management, internet for ordering, automation in production.

Ethical and environmental (page 94)

1. Any three from page 92.

2. Any three from page 92.

3. Advantages and disadvantages given on page 93.

4. To be seen in a positive way by not harming the local environment or community.

5. Ensuring employees are trained, ensuring machinery is kept in good condition and by not overstocking.

6. Recycling, minimising packaging, preventing pollution.

Mackie's Ice Cream case study (page 95)

1. Batch

2. See page 89.

3. Because large numbers of the same product (batch) are produced to a specific recipe.

4. During production – to make sure the correct quantities of ingredients are used.

5. To maximise sales/profit, to satisfy customers, to gain new customers, to increase market share.

6. Mechanisation

7. Make their own tubs, recycling, has wind turbines/solar panels, trains staff.

8. Cuts down on pollution, as tubs no longer have to come from Sweden.

9. Gives a good impression, achieves aim of being socially responsible, increases sales.

10. Any three from pages 85–86 (including justification for each one).

Bluebell Bakery case study (page 96)

1. Any three points (including justifications) from pages 85–86.

2. Sole trader.

3. Cupcakes, cake pops, cakes.

4. Inputs (ie raw materials are taken) and are processed by combining them, cooking them and putting the icing, chocolate, etc. on before the finished product is sold to the customer.

5. Any two from page 92.

6. Advantages and disadvantages of each given on page 93.

7. Making sure the baker knows what they are doing, ensuring machinery (eg oven) is kept in good condition and by not overstocking raw materials/finished products.

8. Two understocking consequences from page 86.

9. Two overstocking consequences from page 87.

10. Using a spreadsheet package that can be easily edited and updated. This will also be good for the environment as it is paper free.

Recruitment and selection (page 108)

1. Recruiting and selecting employees, motivating and training staff, providing safe working conditions, promoting good working relationships, ensuring employees get paid correctly.

2. Recruitment happens before selection – recruitment means getting people to apply for the job and selection means choosing the best person for the job.

3. See diagram on page 105.

4. See pages 106–108.

5. CVs are written by applicant themselves, whereas an application form is given to the applicant to complete (it contains questions the business wants to ask).

6. Recruiting from within the organisation.

7. Recruiting from outwith the organisation.

8. Any 3 from person specification, job description, CV, application form.

Recruitment and selection (page 110)

1. A report from a previous employer or school/college.

2. A meeting between an applicant and people from the business.

3. Any from the table on page 111.

4. Any from the table on page 109.

5. An assessment of a particular skill or aspect of the applicant, eg personality.

6. Any from the table on page 110.

Protest over Further Education cuts – case study (page 116)

1. Demonstration.

2. To raise awareness of the issue.

3. To let people know about funding cuts in further education.

Motivating and retaining (page 116)

1. Induction – given to new employees. On-the-job training takes place in the workplace. Off-the-job training takes place outside the workplace.

2. Any from page 111.

3. Encouraging people to work harder/having a hard-working workforce.

4. Any three from pages 112–113.

5. Know how much will be paid each month.

6. No incentive to work harder.

7. Encourages people to make more sales.

8. Can make employee feel pressured to make sales; stressful.

9. Full time – working 35 hours or more per week whereas part-time is working less than 35 hours per week.

10. Any three from pages 113–114.

11. See page 114.

12. See page 114.

13. See pages 114–115.

14. See table on page 115.

15. Lower productivity, lost orders, unhappy/lost customers, bad image and reputation.

Sources of finance (page 124)

1 and 2: Any three from table on page 124.

Break-even activity (page 129)

Number of cakes	Fixed costs	Variable costs	Total costs	Total revenue	Profit or loss
0	£300	0.00	£300	£0	(£300)
5	£300	£15	£315	£50	(£265)
10	£300	£30	£330	£100	(£230)
15	£300	£45	£345	£150	(£195)
20	£300	£60	£360	£200	(£160)
25	£300	£75	£375	£250	(£125)
30	£300	£90	£390	£300	(£90)
35	£300	£105	£405	£350	(£55)
40	£300	£120	£420	£400	(£20)
45	£300	£135	£435	£450	£15
50	£300	£150	£450	£500	£50

Break-even (page 129)

1. The point at which total revenue = total costs.
2. Costs that do not change with output.
3. Rent, rates, loan repayments, insurance.
4. Costs that do change with output.
5. Raw materials, labour on piece rate, electricity.
6. Total revenue less total costs.

Cash budgeting (page 133)

1. A document that shows expected receipts and payments over a period of time. Used to plan and manage cash flow.
2. To show surplus/deficit, to see if additional finance is needed, to control expenses, to plan/make decisions.
3. Cash expected to be received.
4. More cash coming in than going out.
5. Spending too much on stock, long credit periods for customers, low sales, drawings by owners too high.
6. Getting cheaper suppliers, selling equipment/machinery, arranging additional sources of finance, offering discounts, increasing marketing and promotion.

Technology in finance (page 135)

1. Gross profit is profit from buying and selling, whereas net profit is calculated by taking gross profit and subtracting expenses.

2. Sales less cost of sales (purchases).

3. Rent, advertising, insurance, stationery, electricity, wages.

4. A spreadsheet.

5. Can create graphs, can edit information quickly, can export information to other packages, formulae can be used, statistics can be calculated.